DOES CIVILIZATION NEED
RELIGION?

THE MACMILLAN COMPANY
NEW YORK · BOSTON · CHICAGO · DALLAS
ATLANTA · SAN FRANCISCO

MACMILLAN & CO., LIMITED
LONDON · BOMBAY · CALCUTTA
MELBOURNE

THE MACMILLAN CO. OF CANADA, LTD.
TORONTO

DOES CIVILIZATION NEED RELIGION?

*A Study in the Social Resources
and Limitations of Religion
in Modern Life*

BY

REINHOLD NIEBUHR

NEW YORK
THE MACMILLAN COMPANY
1 9 2 8

SET UP BY BROWN BROTHERS, LINOTYPERS
Printed in the United States of America by
THE FERRIS PRINTING COMPANY, NEW YORK

CONTENTS

DOES CIVILIZATION NEED
RELIGION?

DOES CIVILIZATION NEED RELIGION?

CHAPTER I

THE STATE OF RELIGION IN MODERN SOCIETY

RELIGION is not in a robust state of health in modern civilization. Vast multitudes, particularly in industrial and urban centers, live without seeking its sanctions for their actions and die without claiming its comforts in their extremities. While its influence is still considerable among agrarians and the middle classes of the city, an ever-increasing number of the privileged classes are indifferent to its values. Spiritual and moral forces have always been in a perennial state of decay in those circles of society in which physical ease and cultural advantages combine to make intellectual scruples more pressing than moral ones. But modern scientific education has greatly multiplied the intellectual difficulties of religion and the increasing opulence of

[1]

Western life has rendered its moral problems more perplexing. Industrial workers, in as far as they are socially self-conscious, are almost universally inimical to religion, and their opposition represents a type of anti-religious sentiment which is entirely new in history.

Since the dawn of the modern era the tides of faith have ebbed and flowed so that it is not easy to chart their general course; but it is difficult to escape the conclusion that each new tide has barely exceeded the mark left by a previous ebb. The stream of religious life has been deepened at times, as in the Protestant Reformation, but the impartial observer will note that it has been narrowed as well. A psychology of defeat, of which both fundamentalism and modernism are symptoms, has gripped the forces of religion. Extreme orthodoxy betrays by its very frenzy that the poison of scepticism has entered the soul of the church; for men insist most vehemently upon their certainties when their hold upon them has been shaken. Frantic orthodoxy is a method for obscuring doubt. Liberalism tries vainly to give each new strategic retreat the semblance of a victorious engagement. To retreat from untenable positions is no doubt a necessary step in preparation for new advances; but this necessary strategy has not been accompanied by the kind of spiritual vigor which would promise ultimate victory. The general tendencies toward the secularization of life have been consistent enough to prompt its foes to predict religion's ultimate extinction as a major interest of mankind and to tempt even friendly observers to regard its future with grave apprehension. There are indeed many forms of religion which are clearly vestigial remnants of another day with other interests. They have no vital influence upon the life of modern man, and their continued existence only proves that history, like nature, is slow to destroy what it has found useless, and even slower to inter what it has destroyed. Scattered among the living forms of each civilization are the whitened bones of what was once flesh and blood.

[3]

The sickness of faith in our day may be the senility which precedes death; on the other hand, it may be a specific malady which time and thought can cure. If history is slow to destroy what has become useless, it may be as patient and persistent in reviving what is useful but seems dead. Five hundred years are but a short span in history, and a constant tendency over such a period may lead to premature conclusions. If religion contains indispensable resources for the life of man, its revival waits only upon the elimination of those maladjustments which have hindered it from making its resources available for the citizen of the modern era. Whatever may be said of specific religions and religious forms, it is difficult to imagine man without religion; for religion is the champion of personality in a seemingly impersonal world. It prompts man to organize his various impulses, inherited and acquired, into a moral unity; it persuades him, when its vitality is unimpaired, to regard his fellows with an appreciation commensurate with his own self-respect; and it finally discovers and creates a universe in which the human spirit is guaranteed security against the forces of nature which always seem to reduce it to a mere effervescence unable to outlast the collocation of forces which produced it. The plight of religion in our own day is due to the fact that it has been more than ordinarily pressed by foes on the two lines on which it defends the dignity and value of personality. The sciences have greatly complicated the problem of maintaining the plausibility of the personalization of the universe by which religion guarantees the worth of human personality; and science applied to the world's work has created a type of society in which human personality is easily debased. The pure sciences have revealed a world of nature much more impersonal and, seemingly, much less amenable to a divine will and to human needs than had been traditionally assumed; and the applied sciences have created an impersonal civilization in which human relations are so complex, its groups and units so large, its processes so impersonal, the production of things so important, and ethical action so difficult, that personality is both dwarfed and outraged in it.

Personality is that type of reality which is self-conscious and self-determining. The concept of personality is valid only in a universe in which creative freedom is developed and maintained in individual life as well as in the universe. Religion therefore needs the support of both metaphysics and ethics. It tries to prompt man to ethical action by the sublime assumption that the universe is itself ethical in its ultimate nature whatever data to the contrary the immediate and obvious scene may reveal; and through the cultivation of the ethical life in man it seeks to make such a personalization of the universe both necessary and plausible. It teaches men to find God by loving their brothers, and to love their brothers because they have found God. It inspires a mystical reverence for human personality, prompted by the discovery and creation of a universe in which personality is the supreme power and value; and it persuades men to discover personal values in the universe because they have first come upon clues to the transcendent value of personality in the lives of their fellows. Its ethics is dependent upon its metaphysics and its metaphysics is rooted in its ethics. Religion is thus obviously placed in a desperate plight when its metaphysics and its ethics are imperiled at the same time. It must face and do battle with two hosts of enemies, those who do not believe in men because they do not believe in God, and those who do not believe in God because modern civilization has robbed them of their faith in the moral integrity of men.

Since it is difficult to fight on two fronts at the same time, the forces of religion have been forced to choose one of the two fronts for their major defensive effort. Perhaps it was inevitable that they should choose the easier task. It is easier to challenge the idea of an impersonal universe than to change the fact of an impersonal civilization. That is what the modern church has done and is doing. It is spending all its energy in discounting the

[7]

excessive claims of a deterministic science. It has exhausted its ingenuity in retreating from the untenable positions of an orthodoxy which overstated the freedom and the virtue in the physical universe and therefore aggravated the very determinism by which it was defeated. Outraged truth has a way of avenging itself. The idea of a capricious God working his will in the universe without the restraint of law or the hindrance of any circumstance helped to create the concept of a mechanistic world in which all freedom is an illusion and therefore all morality a sham. Thus the strategic retreats of religion in the field of metaphysics have been the necessary prelude to any new religious advance. Religion may in fact be forced to make some concessions which even modern liberalism seems still unwilling to make. Modern religionists, particularly popular apologists are inclined to add the word creative to the word evolution, and assume that their problem is solved. The modern church has very generally borrowed its apologetic strategy from John Fiske and Henry Drum-

[8]

mond, and has tried to visualize a God who differed from older conception only in this— that he took more time to gain his ends than had once been assumed. The important fact which has escaped many modern defenders of the faith is that the patience of the creative will is a necessary characteristic rather than a self-imposed restraint. There is a stubborn inertia in every type of reality which offers resistance to each new step in creation, so that an emerging type of reality is always in some sense a compromise between the creative will and the established facts of the concrete world. Whether we view the inorganic world, organic life or the world of personal and moral values, each new type of reality represents in some sense a defeat of God as well as a revelation of him. Religious apologetics will probably be forced to concede this fact more generously than has been its wont before it can bring religious affirmations into harmony with scientific facts. Modern liberalism is steeped in a religious optimism which is true to the facts of neither the world of nature nor the

[9]

world of history. The ultimate worth of
human personality in the universe may not be
guaranteed as immediately nor as obviously as
liberal religion seems inclined to assume.
Liberal religion may be forced to discard its
metaphysical and theological monisms, which
have been its support even more than orthodoxy's, and concede that freedom and
creativity in both man and the cosmic order
are more seriously circumscribed than religion
had assumed. But after that concession is
made it is not likely that the idea of freedom,
and the dignity of personality which is associated with it, will ever be completely discredited, whatever may be the deterministic
obsessions of modern science. The various
sciences can momentarily afford to indulge in
their various determinisms because the prestige
of metaphysics as a coördinator of the sciences
has been destroyed for the time being. Each
science is therefore able to disavow the authority of metaphysics and work upon the basis
of its own metaphysical assumptions, which
are usually unreflective and generally deter-

ministic. But the bulk of new knowledge which has momentarily destroyed the authority of any unifying perspective must in time be mastered by philosophical thought; and absolute determinism is bound to be discredited in such a development.[1]

There can be no question but that the development of the physical sciences has permanently increased the difficulty of justifying the personalization of the universe upon which all religious affirmations are based. Every new form of reality is so closely linked to every preceding form out of which it emerges that it is not easy to discern the place where free creativity functions. Yet no total view of reality can ever be permanently mechanistic, for new types of reality do emerge and science is able to explain only the process and not the cause of their emergence.

Important, then, as the metaphysical problem of religion is, it is not the only problem

[1] Professor Alfred Whitehead, in his *Science and the Modern World* and *Religion in the Making,* indicates the inevitable anti-mechanistic trend of philosophical thought as it achieves mastery of the varied fields of modern science.

which it faces. Though it is a real task to reinterpret religious truth in the light of modern science, it is by no means a hopeless one; and though it is necessary, it is not the only necessary task. In the light of modern philosophical inquiries it is justifiable to assume that the most needed hypotheses of religion are metaphysically defensible. In the present situation of religion in civilization, it is more necessary to inquire if and how the peculiar attitudes and the unique life which proceeds from a religious interpretation of the universe may be made to serve the needs of men in modern civilization. The fact is that more men in our modern era are irreligious because religion has failed to make civilization ethical than because it has failed to maintain its intellectual respectability. For every person who disavows religion because some ancient and unrevised dogma outrages his intelligence, several become irreligious because the social impotence of religion outrages their conscience. Religion never lacks moral fruits so long as it has any vitality. It has been placed in such a sorry plight in fulfilling its ethical task in modern civilization because the mechanization of society has made an ethical life for the individual at once more necessary and more difficult, and failure more obvious, than in any previous civilization. If we are not less ethical than our fathers, our happiness is certainly more dependent than that of our fathers upon the ethical character of our society. Rapid means of commerce and communication have brought us into terms of intimacy with all the world without increasing the spiritual dynamic and ethical intelligence which makes such close contact sufferable. We have multiplied the tools of destruction which a confused conscience may wield and have thus armed the world of nature which lives in the soul of man by the same science by which we imagined ourselves to have conquered nature. We have developed so complex a society that it cannot be made ethical by moral goodwill alone, if moral purpose is not astutely guided. Lacking social intelligence, modern civilization has thus robbed man of confidence in his own and his neighbor's moral integrity even when ethical motives were not totally lacking. Civilization with its impersonal and mechanized relationships tends on the one hand to make society less ethical, and on the other to reveal its immoralities more vividly than in any previous age. Religion has a relation to both cause and effect to the moral life. Both its friends and its foes are inclined to judge it by its moral fruits, regarding it as primarily the root, fancied or real, of morality. Yet morality is as much the root as the fruit of religion; for religious sentiment develops out of moral experience and religious convictions are the logic by which moral life justifies itself. In a civilization in which the dominant motives and basic relationships are unethical, religion is therefore doubly affected. The immoralities which bring the reproach of impotence upon it are also the reason for the impotence. Thus modern civilization creates a temper of scorn for a religion which fails to challenge recognized social iniquities, and at the same time it destroys the vitality which religion needs to issue such a challenge. The defection of the industrial workers from religious life and institutions, one of the most significant phenomena of our time, has this double significance. The industrial worker is indifferent to religion, partly because he is enmeshed in relations which are so impersonal and fundamentally so unethical that his religious sense atrophies in him. On the other hand he is hostile to religion because he observes the ethical impotence of the religion of the privileged classes, particularly in its failure to effect improvement in economic and social attitudes. The industrial worker raises a general characteristic of modern urban man to a unique degree. His own experiences help him to see the moral limitations of modern civilization more clearly than do the more privileged classes; but what is true of him is generally true of all members of a complex society in which human relations are impersonal and complicated. If religion is senescent in modern civilization, its social impotence is as responsible for its decline as is its metaphysical maladjustment.

The restoration of its vitality must wait upon the adjustment of its tenets and the reorganization of its life to meet the problems which both the pure and the applied sciences, which both the depersonalization of the universe and the depersonalization of civilization, have created. The metaphysical problem of religion cannot be depreciated. In the long run religion must be able to impress the mind of modern man with the essential plausibility and scientific respectability of its fundamental affirmations. But the scientific respectability of religious affirmations will not avail if the life which issues from them will not help to solve man's urgent social problems. If modern churches continue to prefer their intellectual to their ethical problems, they will merely succeed in maintaining a vestige of religion in those classes which are not sensitive enough to feel and not unfortunate enough to suffer from the moral limitations of modern society. An unethical civilization will inevitably destroy the vitality of the religion of the victims and the sincerity and moral prestige of the religion of the beneficiaries of its unethical inequalities.

The future of religion and the future of civilization are thus hung in the same balance. Both as a means to a moral end and as an end in itself, for which the moral life is the means, the future of religion is involved in the ethical reconstruction of modern society. Social and economic problems are not the only problems which fret the mind and engage the interest of modern men. But they are proportionately more important in an advanced than in a primitive society. Modern men face no problem that is greater than that of their aggregate existence. How can they live in some kind of decent harmony with their fellow men when the size and intricacy of their social machinery tends continually to aggravate the vices which make human life inhuman? How shall they gain mastery over the instruments by which they have mastered nature so that these will not become the means of projecting nature's vices into human history? How shall they bring the life of great social and political groups under the dominion of conscience and moral law? These are the problems upon which hangs the future of civilization. Such social problems are fundamentally ethical and the intimate relation between religion and morality bring them inevitably into the province of religion. Can it help to solve them? Will their solution give religious idealism new vitality? Is the present social impotence of religion due to innate defects? Or is it due to specific and historical limitations which the years may change at least as quickly as they produced them? To such questions we must address ourselves.

CHAPTER II

IT would be extravagant to claim that the possibility of making the resources of religion available for the solution of social problems of modern civilization is absolutely determining for its future. Religion would continue to maintain itself in modern society even if it produced only the scarcest socio-ethical fruits. The problem of living together is not the only problem which men face, and civilization is not the only foe with which personality contends. At least two other fundamental problems engage the interest of every normal individual, that of developing the multifarious forces of his personality into some kind of harmony and unity and that of asserting the dignity and worth of human personality in defiance of nature's indifference and contempt. If religion can render the human spirit a tolerably effective service in the solution of these two problems, its aid will not be scorned though it fail him in his social problem. It will not maintain itself with equal vitality in all strata of society, but it will continue some kind of existence in all of them, and a fairly vigorous life in those classes in which social problems are least urgent.

Psychiatry and the psychological sciences are encroaching upon one service to the perplexed spirit of man which was once an almost exclusive province of religion. They are offering him aid in the task of integrating the heterogeneous forces, with which ages of human and prehuman history have endowed him, into the unity of dependable character; and there are those who think that this service will obviate his need for religion in this field. Undoubtedly it will be to the advantage of any moral or religious discipline of the individual life to avail itself of a more precise knowledge of the intricacies of human personality; yet only the most mechanistic and naturalistic ethical theorist would maintain that the knowl-

edge of self is the only prerequisite of self-
mastery, and that the eternal conflict between
the higher will and the immediate desires, about
which the religious of every age have testified,
may be composed by nothing more than a
better understanding of the devious ways of
human intelligence and emotion. The psychological sciences have undoubtedly saved
men from some morbid fears and repressions,
but the most modern school of psychological
mechanists and determinists seems more
anxious to destroy restraints which are the
product of ages of moral experience than to
correct the defects which reveal themselves
inevitably on the fringe of every moral discipline. The reason mechanistic psychiatry and
psycho-analysis run easily into a justification
of license is because they labor under the
illusion that the higher self (they would scorn
that term) is able to put all internal forces in
their proper place, if only it knows their previous history and actual direction. Under
such an illusion the clamant desires of man's
physical life are bound to be closer to the center

of character than any moral discipline would allow. Modern determinism is too naturalistic to see or to be willing to regard human personality as the incarnation of moral and spiritual values which did not have their origin in any immediate necessity and which no individual will maintain if his resolution is not strengthened by something more than his momentary and obvious experience. This is not to say that moral discipline in individual life can be maintained by religion alone. A humanistic ethical idealism, which makes the experience of the race the guide and inspiration of individual conduct, will not fail to aid men toward some higher integration of personality, though it will seldom go beyond the Greek ideal of a balanced life which knows how to escape sublime enthusiasms as well as crass excesses. The value of religion in composing the conflict with which the inner life of man is torn is that it identifies man's highest values, about which he would center his life. with realities in the universe itself, and teaches him how to bring his momentary impulses

[22]

under the dominion of his will by subjecting his will to the guidance of an absolute will. "Make me a captive, Lord, and then I shall be free," has ever been the prayer of religious people. "He who loses his life for my sake shall find it," said Jesus. In such paradoxes the truth is revealed that the highest peace comes to men where their life is centered not in what is best in them but in that beyond them which is better than their best.

Obviously this function of religion in the life of the individual has its social implications; but it is not to be assumed that the integration of personality automatically solves man's social problem. That assumption, which religion invariably makes, is one of its very defects in dealing with the social problem. A unified personality may still be anti-social in its dominant desires and the very self-respect which issues from its higher integration may become the screen for its unsocial attitudes.

Just as important as the problem of bringing peace to the warring factions within the soul of man is the task of giving human personality a sense of worth in the face of nature's indifference and contempt; and of adjusting man's highest values to nature's sublimer moods. The significance of the religious inclinations of country people lies just here. The peasant is religious because man's relation to the natural world about him is still the agrarian's great interest. His ethical life is simple and develops in those primary or family relationships in which problems are comparatively few and a disturbance of the religious temper by unethical social facts rather infrequent. He is close enough to nature to be prompted to awe and reverence by her beauties and sublimities, to gratitude by her vast and perennial benevolences, and to fear by her occasional cruel caprices. He expresses his awe in worship, his gratitude in the spring and harvest festivals, which are traditional in all religions, and when her momentary atrocities overtake him he appeals from nature's God to the God who is above nature and seeks the intervention of a supernatural ally in behalf of human personality. In a sense the religion of peasants

remains the constant spring of religious sentiment in every class of society, which others
may corrupt or refine but never quite destroy.
Urban men suffer from an atrophy of the
religious sense because they lose, as they are
divorced from the soil, some of the reverence
to which a view of the serene majesties of
nature prompts and some of the fear occa-
sioned by her elemental passions. Yet the most
sophisticated and emancipated city dweller
cannot finally escape the problem of the relation of the human spirit to the natural world
in which it is at once child and rebel. Even
the refinements and artificialities of urban life
will not save man from facing nature's last and
most implacable servant—death, nor free him
of the necessity of making some kind of appeal
against the obvious victory which nature
claims at the grave. The fight of personality
against nature is religion's first battle, and that
is one reason why there is always a possibility
that other struggles will be neglected for it.
Traditional religion fails in its social tasks
partly because men have suffered longer from

the sins of nature than from the sins of man; and religious forms and traditions are therefore better adjusted to offer them comfort for these distresses than for any other from which they suffer. Religion is not yet fully oriented to the new perils to personality which are developed in civilization. But it may fail to meet these and yet not be totally discredited; for the new perils have not supplanted the old ones. At its best religion is both a sublimation and a qualification of the will to live. Defeated by nature the human spirit rises above nature through religious faith, discovering and creating a universe in which divine personality is the supreme power and human personality a cherished, protected and deathless reality. But this religious sublimation of the will to live must be balanced by a qualification of that will to live by which men are persuaded to sacrifice themselves for each other, that they may save themselves from each other and realize their highest self. Love is a natural fruit of religion but not an inevitable one. A high appreciation of personality ought to issue in a reverence for all personalities and in a qualification of the tendency to self-assertion for the sake of other personalities. But left to itself religion easily becomes a force which sublimates but does not qualify man's desire for survival; in which case it may still function in simple societies but will be less useful in those which are highly complex and in which the problem of human relationships has become very important.

Next to the faith of agrarian classes the greatest stronghold of religion is in the life of the middle classes of the city. This phenomenon is due to several causes. Ideals of self-mastery and personal rectitude are always strongest in those classes in which physical resources are not so abundant as to tempt to sensual excesses and not so scant as to lead to an obsession with life's externalities. For that reason the resources of religion for the solution of personal moral problems are particularly coveted by the middle classes. On the other hand the middle classes are also religious because they are comparatively unconscious of their responsibility for society's sins and comparatively untouched by the evil consequences of an unethical civilization. They may therefore indulge in a religion which creates moral respectability, and reinforces self-respect, even though it does not force them to share their sense of worth with all their fellows. There is for this reason an element of hypocrisy in all middle-class religion of which it never becomes clearly conscious but which helps to create the corroding cynicism from which the lower classes of modern society suffer.

Since ideals of personal righteousness flourish in the genteel poverty of the countryside at least as well as in urban middle class conditions, the religion of peasants and the city's middle classes have two characteristics in common: their preoccupation with problems of the individual life and their concern for the adjustment of the soul to nature's realities. But while they share these elements the two types of religion are by no means identical. The simple expedient of claiming divine and supernatural intervention in the soul's specific cases

[28]

of distress does not appeal to the sophisticated intelligence of city people, particularly since higher learning has become so general and science has become the burden of this learning. They are anxious to correct the intellectual inadequacies of traditional religion; and if they are conscious of any moral defects in it, they have the easy faith that these will be eliminated with a proper adjustment of religious affirmations to the world of scientific fact.

The conflict between orthodoxy and liberalism, between fundamentalism and modernism, is essentially a conflict between city and countryside. Though the Protestant Reformation was used by the rising cities to assert the needs of the inner life against a too artificially elaborated institutional religion and to express an ethic of individualism against the traditional loyalties of the peasants rather than to make a readjustment of religion to the growing demands of intellectual life, the humanistic revival which preceded the Reformation was clearly determined by this latter interest and it contributed to the dissolution of the medieval religious structure. In the recent theological controversies within Protestantism, between Conservatism and Liberalism, the religious naïvete of the agrarian and the intellectual sophistication of the city are more obvious influences in the conflict.

The revision of ancient affirmations of faith in the light of modern learning was of course necessary from the point of view of the general needs of the age, and not required merely to satisfy the intellectual scruples of a particular class in society which has a preponderant influence in the Protestant church. It might be better to say therefore that the commercial middle classes appropriated as much as they prompted the revision of Protestant theology and religion.

By doing this they have indeed created a religion capable of maintaining itself in urban civilization, but it develops little power for the ethical reconstruction of industrial society. The same religionists who pride themselves upon the reasonableness of their faith generally use their very modern and revised religion to sanctify a very unmodern and unrevised ethical orthodoxy, an individualistic orthodoxy which makes much of self-realization and comparatively little of the social needs of modern life.

The kind of liberal religion which thrives among the privileged classes of the city gives them some guarantee of the worth of their personalities against the threats of a seemingly impersonal universe which science has revealed, but it does not help to make them aware of the perils to personality in society itself. The final test of any religion must be its ability to prompt ethical action upon the basis of reverence for personality. To create a world view which justifies a high appreciation of personality and fails to develop an ethic which guarantees the worth of personality in society, is the great hypocrisy. It is the hypocrisy which is corrupting almost all modern religion. In a sense hypocrisy is the inevitable by-product of every religion. Men are never as good as their ideals and never as conscious as the impartial observer of their divergence from them. Every religious person commits the error of solipsism in some form or other, the sin of claiming for himself what he will not grant to his brothers. The religion of modern men, particularly of the privileged classes, seems to be more than ordinarily insincere, partly because the social simplicity of another age obscured this inevitable hypocrisy and partly because the privilege of the religious classes is so great and its unethical basis in modern society, particularly from the perspective of the lowly, so patent and so destructive, that it is no longer possible to veil the immoral implications of a self-centered religion.

The question which we really face, therefore, is whether religion is constitutionally but a sublimation of man's will to live or whether it can really qualify the will of the individual and restrain his expansive desires for the sake of society. If it is only the former, it will continue to be the peculiar possession either of those who have no urgent social problems or of those who are the beneficiaries and not the victims of social maladjustments. If religion is

CHAPTER III

THE task of analyzing and isolating the ethical limitations and the social deficiencies of religion is to no purpose if there is not in religion itself, at its best, some resources which civilization and society need for the solution of their problems. Some critics of religion discount it entirely as a social force, or at least as a force of social progress. Bertrand Russell's prejudices on this subject are too violent to make his testimony against religion particularly weighty. Yet he speaks for a large number of ethically sensitive individuals who share his critical attitude, if not his vehemence, when he declares: "Since the thirteenth century the church has consistently encouraged men's blood lust and avarice and discouraged every approach to human and kindly feeling. . . . Emancipation from the churches is still an essential condition of improvement, particularly in America where the churches have more influence than in Europe. . . . Of all requisites for the regeneration of society the decay of religion seems to me to have the best chance of being realized." [1] The number of people among the middle and higher classes who would subscribe to such a denunciation of organized religion is probably not very large. But there are very many who ignore the church as a force for social amelioration; and in the class of industrial workers a temper against the church exceeding even Mr. Russell's violence is very general.

Whatever may be the facts in regard to contemporary religion and to other specific types of organized religious life, it is relevant to ask whether religion as such, freed from its specific limitations, contains indispensable resources for the ethical reconstruction of society.

The first resource which would seem to be of social value is the social imagination which religion, at its best, develops upon the basis of

[1] *Prospects of Industrial Civilization,* page 218.

its high evaluation of personality. A spiritual interpretation of the universe may not issue automatically in a high appreciation of human personality, but religion is never quite able to deny this ethical implication of its faith, and in occasional moments of high insight it revels in it. It persuades men to regard their fellows as their brothers because they are all children of God. It insists, in other words, that temporal circumstance and obvious differences are dwarfed before the spiritual affinities which men have through their common relation to a divine creator. Thus Jesus could deal sympathetically with the harlot of the street, the publican at the gate, the Samaritan woman at the well and the blinded fanatics and their dupes who crucified him. The apostle Paul, though he did not always understand the genius of his master, was nevertheless able to apprehend this central dogma at the heart of religion and declare: "In Christ there is neither Jew nor Greek, neither bond nor free." Celsus, the critic of the Christian church in the first century, derides the church for its failure

[37]

to distinguish between outcasts and respectable citizens. The fervor and consistency with which the church has espoused the ideal of the equal worth of all personalities has not always equaled that of the early church; many compromises with the brute facts of history have been made; yet the church has never been able to betray this faith altogether. The missionary enterprise with all its weaknesses is still a revelation of this power in religion. Oceans are bridged and varying circumstances of race and environment are ignored in order that the soul inspired by God may claim kinship with other souls of every race and every clime.

The physical characteristics and outward circumstances in which men differ are sometimes not so great as they seem to the superficial observer; wherefore education may do as much as religion to cultivate and discover those profounder unities which made all men brothers. There are hatreds which are due merely to misunderstanding. They spring from the parochialism of the average mind, which knows no better than to regard with contempt what differs from the standards and values to which it has become habituated. Education and culture may emancipate men from such hatreds. Other misunderstandings which are caused by a superficial analysis of men's action may be dissipated by a profounder appreciation of the complex life of every individual out of which each action emerges. Yet understanding alone does not solve all the problems of living together. We do not hate only those whom we do not know or understand. Sometimes we hate those most whom we know best. Love does not flow inevitably out of intimacy. Intimacy may merely accentuate previous attitudes, whether they be benevolent or malevolent. Anthropologists are easily obsessed with the inequalities which men reveal in their natural state, and the very abundance of their knowledge prompts them to an ethically enervating determinism when they attempt to gauge the potentialities of so-called primitive peoples. The modern psychologists are more inclined to accept the dogma of the total depravity of man than the ancient theologians were, and they prove thereby that a profound knowledge of human nature need not incline men to regard human beings with reverence and affection. Mr. H. L. Mencken may not speak for the scientists, but he is somewhat typical of the cynicism which follows in the wake of intellectualism. His estimate of human beings is: "Man is a sick fly taking a dizzy ride on a gigantic flywheel. . . . He is lazy, improvident, unclean. . . . Life is a combat between jackals and jackasses." Love is always slightly irrational and requires an irrational urge for its support. It is at least as irrational as hatred and the same intelligence which mitigates the one may enervate the other. A highly sophisticated intelligence is generally unable to survey the human scene with any higher attitude than that of pity for human beings, and pity is a form of contempt under a thin disguise of sympathy.

The facts of human nature are sufficiently complex to validate almost any hypothesis which may be projected into them. Therefore the assumptions upon which we essay our social contacts are all important. One reason why the social sciences can never attain the scientific prestige of the physical sciences to which they aspire is that the importance of hypotheses increases with the complexity and variability of the data into which they are projected. Every assumption is an hypothesis, and human nature is so complex that it justifies almost every assumption and prejudice with which either a scientific investigation or an ordinary human contact is initiated. A vital religion not only prompts men to venture the assumption that human beings are essentially trustworthy and lovable, but it endows them with the courage and inclination to maintain their hypothesis when immediate facts contradict it until fuller facts are brought in to verify it. Mere sentiment is easily defeated by life's disappointing realities. Anatole France observed that if one started with the supposition that men are naturally good and virtuous, one inevitably ends by wishing to kill them all. Human nature is neither lovable nor trustworthy in its undisciplined state and a sentimental overestimate of its virtue may well result in the reaction to which Anatole France alludes. Yet its undeveloped resources are always greater than either a superficial or critical intelligence is able to fathom. There must be an element of faith in love if it is to be creative. "Love," said Paul, "believes all things"; and it may be added that it saves its faith from absurdity by creating some of the evidence which justifies its assumptions. It "hopes till hope creates from its own wreck the thing it contemplates." Nothing less than a religious appreciation of personality, supported by a spiritual interpretation of the universe itself in terms of moral goodwill, will make love robust enough to overcome momentary disappointments and gain its final victory. The injunction of Jesus to his disciples to forgive not seven times, but seventy times seven, represents the natural social strategy of a robust and vital religious idealism, which subdues evil by its unswerving confidence in the good.

While it is true that religion does not issue automatically in an attitude of reverence and goodwill toward all human personalities, it nevertheless remains a fact that a religious world view does incline men to regard their fellow men from a perspective which obscures differences and imperfections and reveals affinities and potential virtue. Even if intelligence became imaginative enough to discover the affinities, it could not be courageous enough to challenge the evil in men in the name of their better selves. The art of forgiveness can be learned only in the school of religion. And it is an art which men must learn increasingly as a complex society makes human associations more and more intimate. Whatever improvement a growing social science may establish in the technique of social intercourse, men will never escape the necessity of overcoming the evil, which they inflict upon each other, by creative patience and courageous trust. A higher intelligence may mitigate our fears and an exacter justice may restrain the inclination to wreak vengeance upon the wrongdoer; but only the stubborn forces of religion will turn fear into trust and hatred into love. Sometimes mutual fear and hatred reduce themselves to such an absurdity (as in the late World War) that even a superficial intelligence can recognize it; but their absurdity does not become patent until they have issued in mutual annihilation. Even then the person with an ordinary commonsense view of life can do no better than to substitute partial trust for fear and partial understanding for hatred. So one war breeds the next. All men are potentially at once our foes and our friends. An unreflective social life assumes that they are enemies and helps to make them so. A higher social intelligence establishes a nicely balanced compromise between trust and mistrust so that the one cannot be very creative and the other not too destructive. Only the foolishness of faith knows how to assume the brotherhood of man and to create it by the help of the assumption. A religious ideal is always a little absurd because it insists on the truth of what ought to be true but is only partly true; it is however

[44]

the ultimate wisdom, because reality slowly approaches the ideals which are implicit in its life. A merely realistic analysis of any given set of facts is therefore as dangerous as it is helpful. The creative and redemptive force is a faith which defies the real in the name of the ideal, and subdues it.

Love is, in short, a religious attitude. There are circumstances in which it may prosper without the inspiration of religion. In the family relation and in other intimate circles proximity and consanguinity may prompt men to regard human beings as essentially good, and direct experience validate their faith. That is why Jesus discounted love in the family as a religious achievement. "If ye love those who love you, what thanks have ye?" In the secondary relations, which are no longer secondary in the matter of importance to human welfare, the matter is not so simple. In these only a sublime assumption will persuade men to embark upon the adventure of brotherhood, and only a robust and constantly replenished faith will inure them against inevitable disappointments. The religious interpretation of the world is essentially an insistence that the ideal is real and that the real can be understood only in the light of the ideal. Since the family relation is the most ethical relation men know, religious faith interprets all life in terms of that relation. In view of many of the facts of history which seem to reveal the world of man as but a projection of the world of nature in which animal fights with animal and herd with herd, this kind of interpretation is superficially too absurd to persuade a highly sophisticated intelligence. It is the truth which is withheld from the wise and revealed to babes. Yet it is the truth without which men will not be able to build a peaceful society. It is the truth which even the physical facts of a highly complex civilization, in which space and time are being annihilated, are conspiring to make true. The races and groups of mankind are obviously not living as a family; but they ought to. And as the necessity becomes more urgent the truth of the ideal becomes more real.

It would be foolish to insist that goodwill alone will create conscience and that to detect the ethical core at the heart of man's being is all that is required to make him ethical. It is a task to persuade human beings to trust their fellows; but is equally important to prompt their fellows to trustworthy action. If human nature is left unchallenged and undeveloped, it hardly qualifies the brute struggle for survival sufficiently to validate any religion or ethic of trust. Men's actions are not as free as we have imagined. The social, economic and psychological sciences have restricted the concept of freedom in the soul of man as the physical sciences have restricted it in the universe. Man is not only less free than he had once imagined, but he is not as free as he once was. If science has discredited the idea of freedom, civilization has circumscribed the fact. It is easier for man to act as an ethical individual in a comparatively simple social group, such as the family, than in a very large and complex social group when even the most robust ethical purpose must meet the resistance and the corruption of the primitive and untamed desires of the group. If man is capable of sacrificing immediate advantages for ultimate ones and his own advantages for the sake of society, this capacity is an achievement which he gains only after much effort and preserves from corruption only at the price of eternal vigilance. The first requisite of an ethical life in modern civilization is a realization of the difficulties which face the human conscience in maintaining itself against the pressure of immediate desires to which the whole emotional life of man is wedded. It is not easy to sacrifice meat for beauty, pleasure for some seemingly ephemeral value, self-interest for the sake of the family, the interest of the family for the sake of society, the interest of our generation for the society of to-morrow. Yet only by such sacrifices can man prove the reality and potency of his creative will. If such sacrifices are not actually made, all so-called morality becomes in fact a device for obscuring the bestiality of man without overcoming it.

The fact that, in spite of the pressure of the struggle for survival, man has created a kingdom of values in which truth, beauty and goodness have been made real, is proof that he is more free and more moral than the modern cynic is willing to concede. But his kingdom of values is never as uncorrupted as he imagines. The task therefore of binding men to spiritual values, and of prompting them to sacrifice immediate pleasures and physical satisfactions for them, is difficult almost to the point of desperation. Religion makes its contribution to it by giving man the assurance that the world of values really has a relevant place in the universe and that values are permanent and will be conserved. He is challenged to sacrifice in a universe in which love is a basic law. He is asked to prefer personal values to property values in a world in which personality is the highest reality. He is prompted to exercise his conscience under the scrutiny and with the sympathy of a higher conscience. Religion in its purest form does not guarantee man an immediate reward for every ethical achievement; indeed it may offer him no reward at all except the reward which inheres in the act itself. But it does give him the final satisfaction of guaranteeing the reality of a universe which is not blind to the values for which he must pay such a high price, and which is not indifferent or hostile to his struggle. It asks him to respect human personality because the universe itself, in spite of some obvious evidence to the contrary, knows how to conserve personality; and to create values in a world in which values are not an effervescence but a reality. Religion is in short the courageous logic which makes the ethical struggle consistent with world facts. In its most vital form religion validates its sublime assumptions in immediate experience and gives man an unshakable certainty. It thus becomes the dynamic of moral action as well as the logic which makes the action reasonable.

The force of its faith operates not only to preserve moral vigor but to sensitize moral judgments. The God of religious devotion is not only revealed in the moral values of the universe outside of man, but he is revealed in the aspirations of man which are beyond his achievements. God insures not only the preservation of values but their perfection. All moral achievement is qualified by the relativities of time and circumstance. The worship of a holy God saves the soul from taking premature satisfaction in its partial achievement. It subjects every moral value to comparison with a more perfect moral ideal. Of course the absolute perfection of God is itself conditioned by the imperfect human insight which conceives it. A cruel age may picture God more cruel than itself, and to a generation lusting for power God may be the supreme tyrant. Thus religion may become the sanctification of human imperfections. Yet in its highest form religion does inculcate a wholesome spirit of humility which gives the soul no peace in any virtue while higher virtue is attainable.

The force of religion in moral action and the necessity of religious assurance for the highest type of social life may be gauged by an analysis of possible alternatives to a social life which is oriented by a religious world view. There are two real alternatives to such a life. The one is based upon an ethical but unreligious world view, and the other scorns both ethics and religion in its absolute determinism. An ethical life which claims no support from religion may on occasion develop a very high type of social idealism, particularly since it escapes the ethical defects of religion even while it sacrifices religious resources. Stoicism is in many respects superior to pantheistic religions; for there are moral advantages in underestimating rather than overestimating the virtue of the universe. It is better to create a sense of tension between the conscience of man and a morally indifferent nature than to obscure the moral defects of nature by a deification of the natural order. But if men disavow all faith in a power not their own which makes for righteousness, they cannot finally save themselves from either arrogance or despair. Religion may destroy man's self-reliance by an undue sense of humility, but

even that limitation is no more destructive of
moral values than a self-reliance which prompts
the human spirit to strut for a while on this
narrow world in the consciousness of unique
virtue before capitulating to a world which is
too blind to know what it has destroyed.
Thomas Huxley thought he would as soon
worship "a wilderness of monkeys" as to give
himself to the worship of humanity after the
fashion of Comte. To insist too strenuously
upon the uniqueness of human life in the cosmic
order must inevitably issue in the pride which
such a worship implies. Since the Renaissance
there has been a marked decay of the spirit of
humility in Western civilization which is closely
associated with the secularization of its ethical
idealism. The difference between the pride of
secular idealism and the humility implicit in
genuine religion may be gauged, as Professor
Irving Babbitt suggests, by comparing Con-
fucius with Buddha and Marcus Aurelius
with Jesus. Pascal thought the stoics were
guilty of "diabolical pride." The judgment
may be too severe, but it must be confessed

[53]

that a purely secular idealism has difficulty in escaping a morally destructive arrogance from which true religion is saved because it subjects all values and achievements to measurement, with its absolutes as the criteria. "Why callest thou me good?" said Jesus: "no one is good save God." In the religion of Jesus the perfection of God is consistently defined as an absolute love by comparison with which all altruistic achievements fall short. "I say unto you, love your enemies; bless them that curse you; do good to them that despitefully use you and persecute you; that ye may be children of your Father in heaven; for he maketh his sun to rise on the evil and the good and sendeth rain upon the just and on the unjust. For if ye love them which love you, what reward have ye? Do not even the publicans the same? . . . Be ye therefore perfect even as your Father in heaven is perfect." [2] Here the value of an absolute standard to save from undue pride in partial ethical achievements is particularly apparent. Prudential morality can

[2] Matthew v. 43-48.

hardly go beyond the encouragement of altruism within the social group, i. e. loving those "which love you." That is precisely what Stoicism did. It is just this pride in partial achievement which complicates the moral problem of modern life; for our ethical difficulties are created by the very tendency of reasonable ethics to make life within groups moral and never to aspire to the moral redemption of inter-group relations. Humility is therefore a spiritual grace which has value not only for its own sake but for its influence upon social problems. Traditional religions, which live off of original inspirations and experiences without recreating them, easily fall into a pride of their own, the pride which comes from identifying the absolute standards of their inspired source with their partial achievements and inevitable compromises. But religion in its purest and most unspoiled form is always productive of a spirit of humility which regards every moral achievement as but a vantage point from which new ventures of faith and life are to be initiated toward the alluring perfection which is in God.

An ethical idealism unsupported by religion is almost as certain to issue in final despair as in unjustified pride. A few choice spirits are sometimes able to imagine themselves in rebellion against the universe without finally succumbing to a temper of sullenness; but the dreadful logic of insisting upon conscience in a conscienceless world inevitably leaves its mark upon the multitude. Oswald Spengler, in his morphology of civilizations,[a] presents "religion without God" as the unvarying symptom of a dying civilization, too sophisticated to believe in the cosmic worth of its moral values but not quite ready to abandon them. The enervating effect of a moral idealism which has sacrificed its hopes with its illusions always becomes apparent in the long run, but frequently it reveals itself quite immediately in the very lives of its most robust champions.

Mr. Russell may think that the "firm foundation of unyielding despair" is an adequate basis for an ethical life, but his own growing bitterness betrays how such a

[a] *The Decline of the West.*

philosophy corrupts moral idealism with a sense of frustration. The idealist is put into the position of sacrificing everything for values which have no guaranteed reality in the cosmic order. Even his faith in mankind is finally destroyed; for however precious personal values may seem in a given moment, his philosophy denies him the right to attribute any lasting worth to them. True religion gives man a sense of both humility and security before the holiness which is at once the source and the goal of his virtue; and thus it saves him at the same time from premature complacency and ultimate despair. The choice between irreligious and religious idealism is the choice between pride which issues in despondency and humility which becomes the basis of self-respect. There is an irrational element in either alternative; but the irreligious idealist is in error when he imagines that he has chosen the more reasonable alternative; his choice is no more reasonable and morally much less potent.

The absolute determinists who have as little

confidence in the moral integrity of human nature as in any moral meaning in cosmic facts are more consistent than the Stoics, but they are involved in worse absurdities. Their cynicism robs them of both an adequate motive and an adequate method for social reconstruction. Discounting moral idealism even while they exhibit it in their social passion, they ostensibly desire social reconstruction only in the interest of the class to which they belong. But their personal interests are not frequently identical with those of the oppressed classes and they are moved as much by sympathy for the plight of the victims of our present society as by any selfish considerations. They profess to be prompted by the reflection that individual action has become useless in a capitalistic age and that it is possible to advance the interests of an individual only by making common cause with other individuals in a similar predicament. Meanwhile there is hardly an economic determinist, even among those who are actually members of the class of the oppressed, who could not gain higher advantages for him-

self by disassociating himself from his class
than by making common cause with it. This
is certainly true of those who are intelligent
enough to evolve or elaborate the theory of
absolute determinism.

Absolute determinism, when developed consistently, must disavow all other methods of
social reconstruction but that of ruthless conflict. If nothing qualifies the self-interest of
men, a conflict of interests becomes inevitable.
This defect in method is even more important
than the defect in its motive. A ruthless
struggle can result in an ordered society only
if the victors are able to annihilate their foes.
But even in that event the interests of the
members of any class engaged in a social or
political struggle will cease to be identical as
soon as its foes are eliminated. Thus a new
and equally ruthless struggle must result
between the comparatively strong and comparatively weak, the comparatively privileged
and the comparatively underprivileged victors.
Ultimately men cannot escape the necessity
of building a stable society by the mutual

compromise and the mutual sacrifice of conflicting rights. The determinists have made
an important contribution to the modern
social problem by revealing the brutal nature
of much of man's social life. Even if the
human conscience could be sensitized to a much
greater degree than now seems probable, it
will not be possible to eliminate conflict
between various social and economic groups.⁴
Good men do not easily realize how selfish they
are if someone does not resist their selfishness;
and they are not inclined to abridge their
power if someone does not challenge their right
to hold it. Religious and moral idealism cannot be expected to eliminate, but it can be

⁴ Stuart Mill's refutation of LePlay's thesis that the salvation of the working classes can come only through the benevolence of their superiors is worth quoting in this connection:
"No times can be pointed out in which the higher classes of
this or any other country performed a part even distantly
resembling the one assigned to them in this theory. All
privileged and powerful classes have used their power in the
interest of their own selfishness. I do not affirm that what
has always been must always be. This at least seems to be
undeniable, that long before superior classes could be sufficiently inspired to govern in the tutelary manner supposed,
the inferior classes would be too much improved to be
governed."

expected to mitigate social warfare. The conscience of man must finally be the force which
builds a new society; and a man with a conscience must be the end for which such a society
is built. If there is no virtue in man which lifts
him above the brute struggle for survival,
there is no value in him to justify the effort of
building a new and more perfect society—and
he is not the stuff out of which such a society
can be built. It is difficult to escape the conclusion that the reverence for personality
which is implicit in religion is necessary to
establish an adequate motive and an adequate
method of social reconstruction. Reverence
for personality qualifies the individual's will to
power so that his life can be integrated with
other lives with a minimum of conflict; and it
saves society from sacrificing the individual to
the needs of the group. In the religion of
Jesus both a social and an individualistic
emphasis issues from a spiritual appreciation
of human personality. The individual is given
a place and prestige which he never before possessed in society. Western civilization owes

much to the high evaluation of the individual which Jesus introduced into the thought of the world. On the other hand this emphasis is saved from mere individualism by an ethic which helps the individual to realize his highest self by sacrificing personal advantages for social values.

The contribution of religion to the task of an ethical reconstruction of society is its reverence for human personality and its aid in creating the type of personality which deserves reverence. Men cannot create a society if they do not believe in each other. They cannot believe in each other if they cannot see the potential in the real facts of human nature. And they cannot have the faith which discovers potentialities if they cannot interpret human nature in the light of a universe which is perfecting and not destroying personal values.

CHAPTER IV

THE SOCIAL CONSERVATISM OF MODERN RELIGION

THE charge against religion most frequently
made by critics who are interested in social
reconstruction is that it is a conservative force
which impedes social progress. If it has
resources which are indispensable for the life
of society, social idealists will not appreciate
them if its contemporary forms are invariably
aligned with the social forces most intent upon
preserving the status quo. Contemporary liberal Christianity refutes the charge of social
conservatism by appealing to the social
radicalism of Jesus which it alleges to have
appropriated. By this appeal liberal Christianity exhibits one of the very tendencies of
religion which subjects it to the criticism of
social liberals. Religion is easily tempted to
make devotion to the ideal a substitute for its
realization and to become oblivious to the

inevitable compromise between its ideal and the brute facts of life. The absolute nature of the ethics of Jesus and the perfect harmony between his religion and his ethics may be the guarantee of the perennial spiritual and ethical renewal of the Christian religion; but it is also occasion for the self-deception of many professed disciples. Many streams of thought have contributed to the current of modern liberal Christianity and it contains alluvial deposits from all Western civilizations. Yet it imagines that it represents a simple return to radical and dynamic ethics of the religion of Jesus. By this deception it easily becomes the façade behind which the brutal facts of modern industrial civilization may be obscured rather than a force by which they might be eliminated. The Protestant Reformation suffered from the same deception. It thought of itself as a return to the original ideal when it was, as a matter of fact, a new type of compromise.

Catholicism was a compound of early Christianity and the thought and life of Græco-Roman civilization. The medieval church was a kind of ghostly aftermath of the Roman empire and the popes were inspired by the genius of Cæsar as much as by the spirit of Christ. The north European peoples first accepted this latinized Christianity, partly because they were attracted by those universal elements in it which have made their appeal to all peoples, and particularly those of the Western world, and partly because it was for them the symbol of the ordered civilization of Rome which they first envied, then destroyed, and finally tried to rebuild. In time they reacted against the ecclesiastical, international and feudal solidarities of this whole politico-religious world, prompted no doubt by the untamed spirit of liberty which characterized the northern peoples and which resented the tyranny by which the middle ages achieved their high measure of social cohesion. Thus Protestantism became the handmaiden of a budding nationalism which was impatient of the restraints of an international papacy, as it has since been impatient of every other type of international control. In time it also came to be the peculiar spiritual possession of those classes among the northern peoples who developed modern commerce and industry. The affinity between its sanctification of the principle of liberty and the necessary individualism of classes which were intent upon destroying the traditional restraints of the ancient world for the sake of giving unhampered play to a growing commercial and industrial life, has been so perfect that it is hardly possible to decide which of the two is cause and which effect. Max Weber [1] has made an interesting analysis of commercial and industrial superiority of Protestant nations. It may be that the aptitude for commercial and industrial pursuits and an inclination to the Protestant form of the Christian faith are concomitant characteristics of north European peoples rather than casually related phenomena. Yet they have become so intimately related in history that the most typical commercial classes and nations are most generally Protestant, and most uniquely Protestant. In England the

[1] *Gesammelte Aufsaetze zur Religions-Sociologie.*

nonconformist sects are almost identical with the commercial middle classes, while the established church with its semi-Catholic genius has spiritual affinities both with the old Tories and the new world of the industrial worker. In Germany there is a similar alignment with Catholic and agrarian Bavaria on the one hand and the highly industrialized and Protestant Prussia on the other. The contrast between Protestant and industrial Ulster and Catholic and agrarian south Ireland is equally significant. Everywhere in Western civilization, and nowhere more than in America, Protestantism with its individualism became a kind of spiritual sanctification of the peculiar interests and prejudices of the races and classes which dominate the industrial and commercial expansion of Western civilization.

Since liberal Christianity is the product of an adjustment of the main tenets of orthodox Protestantism to the sophistication of the cities and the growing intelligence of the privileged and therefore educated classes, its whole moral atmosphere is much more determined by the special interests of these classes than it is willing to admit. The authority of Jesus, to which it appeals, has indeed been given a new emphasis, but this has been done because liberal Christianity valued the theological simplicity rather than the moral austerity of his gospel. In the same way many liberal Jews have appealed from the law to the prophets, not because they had a great passion for the ethical rigors of an Amos or Isaiah but because they found obedience to the minute exactions of the law too onerous in a sophisticated age. Jesus is valuable to the modern Christian because he offers an escape from the theological absurdities of the ancient creeds; meanwhile his ethical and religious idealism will not leave the lives of those who profess to follow him unaffected. In time it may become the instrument of the regeneration of Western society; but this will not be possible if the liberal church does not overcome its self-deception and realizes that its religious and moral life is a composite into which have entered the imperialism of Rome, the sophistication of the Greeks, the fierce tribalism and individualism of the Nordics and the prudential ethics of an industrial civilization.

Religion can be healthy and vital only if a certain tension is maintained between it and the civilization in which it functions. In time this tension is inevitably resolved into some kind of compromise. The tendency of religion to become a conservative social force is partly derived from its ambition to defend the resultant compromise in the name of its original ideal. Thus all partial values, determined by geographic, economic, social and political forces, are given a pseudo-absolute character by the religious elements which entered into the compromise; and their defects are sufficiently obscured and sanctified to make them comparatively impregnable to the attacks of the critics of the status quo. The Russian moujik was more than ordinarily docile under the tyranny of the czars and more than ordinarily patient with the imperfections of his society, because his obedience was claimed not by Russia but by "holy Russia," the historic incarnation of his religion. In the same way the medieval church became organically involved with feudalism and forced the critics of feudal society to undermine its influence before they could hope to change the feudal social order. Orthodox Protestantism is intimately related to this day with Nordicism, with the racial arrogance of north European peoples. The Ku Klux Klan, which thrives in the hinterlands of America, maintains its influence over simple minds by screening racial prejudice against Slavic, Latin and Semitic peoples behind a devotion to the spiritual treasures of Protestantism and their defense against the fancied peril of allegedly inferior religions. In Ireland the racial pride of Ulstermen expresses itself in a passionate espousal of the Presbyterian religion and a contemptuous attitude toward the Catholicism of the Irish. In modern pre-war Germany there was a curious partnership between "Thron und Altar," the interests of the nationalist German state, as integrated by the Prussian royal house, with the interests of Protestantism. To this day the fanatic

monarchists of Germany are also Protestant
extremists who imagine that the monarchy was
undermined by religiously motivated conspiracies of Jews and Catholics. Incidentally
the Lutheran type of Protestantism which
flourishes in Germany has always been less
intimately aligned with the commercial classes
than the Calvinistic sects of other Western
nations. While the German socialists include
the Lutheran church among the forces of reaction with which they must contend, the church's
real strength is among the peasants and junk-
ers, who are also the strongest support of
monarchist opinion and who abhor the demo-
cratic liberalism of commercial and industrial
Germany as much as they despise socialist
radicalism; and they imagine both to be
inspired by Semitic designs upon their national
integrity. The real inspiration of this liberalism with its emphasis on international conciliation and coöperation is born out of the
economic and political necessities of an industrial and commercial state which cannot afford
to indulge in the fanatic nationalism to

which peasants and agrarian aristocrats are prone.

Liberal Christianity as it has developed in the urban centers of the Western world grew out of the intellectual and religious needs of the privileged classes and bears the marks of its social environment just as much as the other types of religion which have preceded it and with which it is historically related. It is in the same danger of becoming a spiritual sublimation of the peculiar interests and prejudices of these classes while it imagines itself the bearer of an unconditioned message to its day. It has preserved the same individualistic ethics which has characterized orthodox Protestantism and which is so dear to the hearts of the commercial classes, and so unequal to the moral problems of a complex civilization in which the needs of interdependence outweigh the values of personal liberty. The supposed devotion of the privileged classes to a religion in which the sacrifice rather than the stubborn preservation of individual rights is enjoined and in which the prudential and utilitarian root of morality

intelligence which computes selfish advantage which may flow from moral action is not imaginative enough to include all persons who are affected by an action and not dynamic enough to balance the drive of self-interest which influences it.

In modern industrial society those who are in position of power and privilege are most inclined to espouse an ethical ideal because it tends to stabilize social life and thus insures the perpetuation of privilege. They are also most easily tempted to restrict ethical action so that it will prompt to no sacrifices which are not consistent with a wise self-interest. Since they are also the classes which have, for reasons previously discussed, maintained their loyalty to religion, the church can avoid connivance with their prudential morality only by a continual regeneration of its religious life. Failing to maintain a distinction between utilitarian ethics and a religiously inspired moral life, the church cannot escape the fate of becoming a useful adjunct of the forces of privilege in the social and economic conflict in which modern society is engaged. It may be good business to pay high wages, but social good may demand an increase in the wages of workers beyond the point where economic advantage is derived from an enlightened wage policy. It may be wise to share some privileges so that all of them will not be lost, but sensitive ethical insight will detect the selfishness and insincerity in such a course. A religion which sanctifies such social prudence is ultimately a hindrance to the ethical reconstruction of modern society. A religion which discovers and amends the limitations of prudential morality by the elements of its reverence for personality and its quest for the absolute is a necessary factor in social reconstruction.

The question which faces the modern church is whether it will help to hide or to discover the limitations in the ethical orientation of modern life. Its devotion to the gospel of Jesus may serve either purpose. The contempt for ethical opportunism implied in the whole idealism of Jesus and its scorn for immediate advantages are the very ethical values which the generation needs, but they are also the values which have given the Christian religion its great moral authority and prestige which the church can so easily misuse. If the authority of Jesus prompts men to a courage and imagination which escapes the defects of contemporary morality, its influence will be redemptive; if it is used merely to hide the defects, the critics of the church will be justified in regarding it as detriment to social progress. The religion which is socially most useful is one which can maintain a stubborn indifference to immediate ends and thus give the ethical life of man that touch of the absolute without which all morality is finally reduced to a decorous but essentially unqualified self-assertiveness. The paradox of religion is that it serves the world best when it maintains its high disdain for the world's values. Its social usefulness is dependent upon its ability to maintain devotion to absolute moral and spiritual values without too much concern for their practical, even for their social usefulness. The church is in a very favorable position to make a necessary contribution to social life, for it reveres as Lord one whose life incarnates the strategy which saves morality from insincerity. But its assets easily became moral liabilities when it compounds the pure idealism of Jesus with the calculated practicalities of the age and attempts to give the resultant compromise the prestige of absolute authority.

CHAPTER V

RELIGION AND LIFE: CONFLICT AND COMPROMISE

IT is obvious that the ethical potency of
religion depends largely upon its ability to
make its ideals effective in the world and yet
preserve a measure of detachment from those
natural forces which express themselves in
human society and offer such stubborn resistance to every spiritual and ethical ideal that
no victory has yet been gained over them in
which the heel of the victor has not been
bruised. Ideal religion makes reverence for
personality the end of human action. Society
has its various secular ends the attainment of
which necessitates the debasement of personality. Religion seeks to persuade men to
sacrifice immediate advantages for ultimate
values; the average man whose influence is
dominant in all large social groups is not easily
persuaded to forego immediate and concrete

[79]

advantages for values which are too remote and too ephemeral to captivate his imagination. There must therefore be a tension between the spiritual ideal and all historic societies. The significance of Jesus for the religious life of the Western world is due to his attainment and incarnation of a spiritual and moral ideal of such absolute and transcendent nature that none of his followers have been able to compromise it by their practical adjustments to the social necessities of their day. There is therefore a resource in the avowed loyalty of Western civilization to his ideal which may yet become the basis of its redemption. It is the peculiar characteristic of men and societies, and an evidence of both their moral and immoral nature, that they reserve their most unqualified devotion for those ideals and personalities which they find difficult to realize or emulate. They pay tribute to the ideal even while they are corrupting it and they reward those who have accommodated it to their indifferent capacities with a more qualified respect.

It was probably inevitable that the church

should adjust the spiritual ideal, which to propagate it ostensibly regards as its very raison d'être, to the practical needs of the various ages and social orders with which it came in contact. But it is necessary that it should be shrewd enough to see the compromise involved in every adjustment and be stubborn enough to make a new bid for victory after every partial defeat. On the whole the Catholic church, which Protestants easily assume to have been more amenable to the practical demands of an unregenerate society than the churches of the Reformation, has really been much shrewder than these in gauging the hazards to virtue in the most natural social relationships. Some of the moral weaknesses in the modern church may be traced directly to the naïvete of Protestantism in dealing with the vagaries of human nature, and in failing to estimate the overt and covert peril to its values in the ordinary ways of men.

Medieval Catholicism had various strategies in preserving and relaxing the tension between

the ideal of religion and the practical needs of
men and society. It made fewest demads upon
the individual. He was permitted to indulge
almost all the natural appetites and ambitions
which characterize the life of the average man.
For him the religion of the church was a magic
which guaranteed divine intervention in critical moments and which offered a rather easy
short-cut to the prizes of the spirit which ought
to be won only by virtuous achievement. Yet
this same church had an uncompromising attitude toward the various social institutions
which Protestantism has never equaled. It
insisted on the sacramental nature of the family
union with such intransigeance that it may
fairly be accused of failing to make necessary
accommodations of its spiritual ideal to the
imperfections of human nature. It dealt with
economic relations with less severity but
enforced ethical ideals upon them which must
seem unusually exacting to an age which has
become accustomed to the connivance of Protestantism with laissez-faire economics. The
master of the medieval church, Thomas

Aquinas, had elaborated a theory of the just price for all commercial transactions, which the church made every effort to apply and which it enforced through the canonical law. The church did not organize the guilds but it blessed them; and their efforts to regulate wages, fix fair profits, insure high quality of merchandise and organize mutual aid among their members were prompted by a religiously inspired moral idealism. While it dealt less successfully with the ethical implications of the relations between landowners and peasants, it impressed the owners with a sense of their obligation toward those who were economically dependent upon them which to this day gives the landed aristocracy of European nations a certain moral superiority over the industrial overlords who have been trained in more modern schools of thought. The ambition of the medieval church to dominate the life of the nations is well known but frequently misinterpreted. The contest between the papacy and the empire was indeed in some of its aspects no more than a conflict between two great political organizations lusting for the power which easily becomes the sole end of the life of social and political organisms. Yet there was a measure of ethical idealism in the political aspirations of the popes to which Protestant thought has given scant justice. In the two greatest exponents of the papacy as an international political force, Gregory VII and Innocence III, particularly in Gregory, the ethical ideal of a unified Christian society which knows how to hold the capricious self-will of nations in check and how to set bounds to their natural lust for power is of no small moment in the development of papal policy. The very autocracy of the papacy, which the modern world finds so little to its liking, was elaborated by Gregory in order to save the church from international anarchy and make it an instrument of international unification. Incidentally Gregory was neither the first nor the last great statesman who preferred autocracy to anarchy, and the preference is supported by more than one lesson of history. Free coöperation between individuals and groups is a high and rare political and moral achievement, and where men's capacities are unequal to it there are occasions when it may be better to sacrifice freedom than to destroy social cohesion. At any rate the medieval church revealed both political shrewdness and spiritual idealism in its attempt to dominate the life of nations. Naturally its efforts did not result in any ideal society. The ambition of the Cæsar haunted the life of the popes and in many respects the work of their hands approximated the dominion of an Augustus more nearly than the kingdom of God of Christian dreams. The Christian ideal of an ethical international society was thus corrupted by imperial ambition in its very inception, and the historical realities which sprang from it diverged even farther from any conceivable ideal. Yet the whole political policy of the medieval church is in marked contrast to the easy capitulation of historic Protestantism before the force of economic and political groups. If Catholicism's treatment of the moral problems of the individual represents the relaxation of the tension between religion and life, and its social and political policy represents the compromise which follows inevitably upon the conflict of the ideal with the moral inertia of life, its monasticism represents the strategy of religion when it seeks to maintain an absolute tension between its ideal and historic reality.

The various ascetic movements which prospered under the general ægis of the medieval church represent so many different types of religious idealism that no generalization about them will be accurate. Protestantism reacted violently from the monastic ideal and therefore has been able to see nothing in monasticism but a selfish flight from life's realities. Monasticism may be a retreat from life, but at its best it was not a selfish retreat. Its development of the arts, its emphasis on learning, its vast philanthropies and its religious zeal for those outside of the monastic walls are not selfish characteristics. It did sometimes degenerate into a very odious type of spiritual selfishness and pride; but if we judge it by its

[86]

typical exemplars, we cannot accuse it of a lack of social passion. The religious fervor of Catholic ascetics has been matched by Protestant mystics, but their ethical insights have never been excelled. Their superior moral shrewdness was revealed in their ability to detect the perils to the ethical ideal which are covert in the natural and, from any obvious perspective, virtuous social relationships. They saw that the family, in itself the most virtuous of human groups, could easily become the occasion for disloyalty to high fealties of the soul. "Whoso loveth father or mother more than me is not worthy of me," Jesus had said, and no one in the history of the church seems to have understood the problem with which he dealt in those words as well as Catholic ascetics. It must be said that the celibacy of the monasteries was not prompted solely by the desire to avoid conflicting loyalties; it sprang partly from a morbid evaluation of the sexual relation. That was probably the weakest and least worthy characteristic of medieval ascetism. Its understanding of the perils to the spirit in the possessive instinct was perhaps its finest bit of insight. It understood how easily the privilege and power which spring from the possession of property may corrupt the soul with pride and destroy a loving relationship between individuals. It therefore insisted upon the vow of poverty. In all these problems the insight of asceticism was superior to its strategy. It saw peril in ordinary human relationships where most modern Christians are unable to detect them; but it knew of no way to overcome the peril except by destroying the relationships and building its unique fellowship of the spirit upon the basis of celibacy, poverty and absolute obedience. In asceticism the flowers of the spirit are cut from the roots by which they are supported and life is destroyed in the process of its purification. Asceticism creates a high type of ethical spirituality which cannot be universalized without completely destroying society; and the virtue which it develops can be maintained only in its own artificial media and therefore lacks redemptive force. The great medieval ascetics have always claimed Jesus as their authority though he was not an ascetic in their sense. He disassociated himself from the asceticism of John the Baptist, who had come "neither eating nor drinking," and unlike the ascetics he had no morbid fears of natural enjoyments. Protestantism has therefore regarded asceticism as the result of a foolish literalism which failed to allow for poetic latitude in the words of Jesus. Nevertheless it must be admitted that both his words and his practice have a closer affinity to medieval asceticism at its best than to any modern spiritualized worldliness which tries vainly to unite the largest number of spiritual graces with the greatest possible temporal advantages. Francis of Assisi was surely more like the real Jesus than Bruce Barton's modernized caricature of the original. The strategy of Jesus might be described as a leaning in the direction of asceticism, as a hovering upon its brink. He is saved from its morbid temper by the wholesome common sense which leavens all his attitudes. The virtue of asceticism lies in its ability to detect the perils to a virtuous life in the necessary and inevitable social relationships in which all individual personality must develop; its limitation is its inclination to destroy the relationships in order to overcome the peril. Religious idealism, nurtured in the individualism of Protestantism, fails to appreciate the virtue of asceticism, while it condemns its limitations because it fails to realize how fundamentally all individual ethical achievements are qualified by the society in which men live. Wherever that fact is fully understood, every honest effort to maintain the purity of the religious ideal will result in strategies which will approximate asceticism at many points and which may excel it only in the ability to avoid its depreciation, occasionally morbid depreciation, of the ordinary functions of life.

Protestantism's reactions to the problems of preserving a sense of tension between religion and life have been a little more varied than those of the medieval church because of the multifarious nature of its historic forms. But varied as may be the strategies of the various churches, they do not finally differ from the three which Catholicism employed, i.e., capitulation without a struggle, compromise after a struggle, and victory gained through the device of avoiding some of the issues. The marked differences between the medieval and the modern church lie in the areas of life where the struggle between religion and human inertia was attempted, where the compromises were made and where the victories were won. If Catholicism left the individual to his own devices, the churches of the Reformation followed a similar course in dealing with the moral problems of all human groups. The state was completely secularized under Protestant influence. The Reformation was in some of its aspects simply a simultaneous revolt of the various new nations of Europe against the restraints of the international papacy. In Germany, Scotland and finally in England, the nationalistic motive was a decided force in destroying the prestige of the old religion. Lutheranism capitulated much more easily to the secular state than Calvinism, which tried in fact to maintain the ancient controls upon political life. But once the Reformation had destroyed the old unity of Western society and the prestige of the organization which maintained it, secular nationalism became the universal characteristic of Western civilization. Even Calvinism, which was ambitious to dominate the policy of political states, hardly had the opportunity of affecting international relations. Its influence barely went beyond domestic policy, and there it was less interested in the morality of the state than in the legal enforcement of individual moral ideals. The greed and lust for power of national groups is not a unique characteristic of the modern world; but our own era takes the moral autonomy of the nation for granted more generally than did the Middle Ages. The Protestant church did not create Machiavellian politics but it was more impotent before unscrupulous nationalism than any other institution of the religious ideal, and its impotence was partly due to its lack of interest in social problems.

The emancipation of economic relations

from all ethical restraint was more or less concomitant with the Reformation movements,
but it is a question how much it was causally
and how much coincidentally related. Tawney [1] thinks that the growing complexity of
commercial transactions invalidated the old
canonical laws designed to enforce ethical
standards in business, and thus made the
secularization of economics inevitable even
before the Reformation. Luther and Calvin
were as anxious as the fathers of the medieval
church to preserve moral standards in business.
But they were no more ingenious than these in
devising new and more flexible methods of
control when the prohibition of usury and the
fixation of a just price were swept away by a
growing commerce which made money-lending
an incident of commercial enterprise rather
than a philanthropic device, and which
engulfed the standards by which a just price
was determined in a sea of economic relativities. Luther was completely baffled by the
intricacies of the new world and could do little

[1] *Religion and the Rise of Capitalism.*

more than try vehemently but futilely to maintain the old prohibition against usury and insinuate meanwhile that the recently developed system of international banking was in some mysterious way related to the evil conspiracies of the papacy. Calvinism, true to its genius, was more ambitious in dealing with the problems of commerce; so much so in fact that Beza's thunderous denunciations of covetousness prompted the Geneva Council to declare that he stirred up class hatred against the wealthy. Yet it was Calvin who finally destroyed the last vestige of medievalism in economics by justifying interest. Though his action prompted the charge that "usury was the brat of heresy," he probably did no more than to recognize the logic inherent in the facts of a new economic development. There was no more conscious desire to emancipate commercial life from the sanctions of morality and religion in Protestantism than in the ancient church; but the preoccupation of the leaders of the Reformation with the problem of the inner life and the general temper of individualism which characterized the Protestant churches undeniably accelerated the processes of secularization. In time Adam Smith rather than Thomas Aquinas became the moral authority of the commercial world, and, whatever may have been the futile fury of the early reformers, Protestantism did finally accept the economics of laissez faire and habituated itself to a world in which vast areas or life were withdrawn not only from the influence of religiously inspired ethical ideals, but from every ethical sanction whatsoever. Thus was the present world created in which "business is business" and "politics is politics," i.e., in which the non-moral character of two of the most important social relationships of mankind is taken for granted.

If Protestantism made its easy capitulation before the larger social groups of mankind and its premature peace with them, it developed its most stubborn resistance to the natural appetites of men in its influence upon the individual life. It was precisely in that area of life in which the medieval church was least effective that Protestantism displayed its highest ambition. At this point it becomes impossible to speak in general terms of Protestantism, for the strategies of Calvinism and Lutheranism in dealing with the problems of the inner life differ widely, even more widely than their social policies. The unique characteristics of either are frequently the common characteristics of Protestantism when viewed from some external perspective; but an intimate view may reveal them in the light of very different religions. Calvinism is religion's most energetic effort to master the ethical life of the individual. In some of its historic forms, in Geneva and Scotland and the American colonies for instance, its social policy was ambitious enough to compare with that of Pope Gregory, but its chief interest was not in the social institution as such. It merely used the political power to reinforce an uncompromising ethical rigor in the life of the individual. In Calvinism the religion of the modern world makes its boldest bid for the ethical mastery of life. Calvinism believed that life could be dominated by the spiritual and ethical ideal if the individual could be persuaded to control his appetites and to overcome his natural indolence. A temperate, industrious, thrifty and honest individual was, in its esteem, the perfect exemplar of the religious ideal and the stuff out of which a new society could be built. It never faced the problem of the conflict between the ideal in the soul of the individual and the intractable forces in human society because its moral ideals were socially and economically very useful and it could therefore indulge the illusion that economic success, social well-being and obvious happiness are the natural and inevitable fruits of the religious life. Hence it was a religion admirably suited for the middle classes who rose to power in the seventeenth, eighteenth and nineteenth century, for it endowed them with virtues which would insure their success and it doubled their zeal by giving religious sanction to their secular enterprises. The ancient and medieval world had given moral precedence to a life of leisure and meditation, whether of aristocrat or philosopher, of monk or priest. Calvinism was as contemptuous of luxury and leisure as of the arts and amenities which flourished in them. Its sanctification of the common task, of manual toil and of commercial enterprise was in itself a valuable contribution to social progress. It was in a way the spiritual foundation upon which the whole structure of modern civilization has been built. It developed a high type of honesty without which the intricate credit relationships of modern commerce would have been impossible. It encouraged a diligence which was the driving force in establishing the commercial classes in power over a moribund aristocracy. Its religiously inspired habits of continence and temperance gave the lower classes a sense of moral dignity and a natural self-respect which they needed in challenging the pride and complacency of the aristocratic world. These puritan virtues have moreover given the whole north European world and America (which is more puritan than any nation, because here the puritan life flourished on virgin soil and

[98]

remained unqualified by the vestiges of medievalism which remain firmly imbedded in the culture of even the most modern European nations) a robust vitality and moral urge which have had no small part in developing their political hegemony in the modern world.

The conflict of puritan religion with the world has however resulted in the inevitable compromise between the religious ideal and the world's primitive urges and desires. Its moral weakness lies in its naïve confidence of victory over the world and its inability to discover the relativities and qualifications which history has wrought upon its absolute. If the spiritual idealism of Jesus is the norm for Christians, the Calvinists and puritans diverged from it more seriously than they knew in the very conception of their ideal. The love and reverence for personality which is the basis of the ethics of Jesus is totally lacking in Calvinism. It knows how to create self-respect but lacks the imagination to inculcate a religious respect for others, except possibly for the respectable. Its confidence in the obvious rewards of virtue tempted it to abhor poverty and hold the poor in contempt, though they might become the helpful occasion for the exercise of that philanthropy without which the idea of Christian stewardship could not be realized. While early Calvinism had an heroic mood which would have scorned to make a concession to the selfishness of man through the sanctification of prudential ethics, its ethical theories did nevertheless lend themselves to easy appropriation by moralists who were intent upon identifying the social good with a decent selfishness. The uncompromising spirituality of the ethics of Jesus is totally lacking in Calvinism. Its moral theories were in fact derived from the Old rather than the New Testament; and there is hardly a scintilla of evidence in Calvinistic thought that the Sermon on the Mount is recorded in the scripture which it accepted as revealed finality. Its very bibliolatry was partly responsible for its non-Christian type of ethics, for through it the casual moral theories of the early Hebrews achieved the dignity of absolute truth. Lack of historical per-

spective in the use of the Old Testament further aggravated this error, for the real worth
of the prophets was never appreciated and their
high type of moral idealism could not serve
to qualify the less heroic morality of the law
and the superficial moralizing of the Wisdom
literature. Incidentally it may be observed
that bibliolatry is one of the handicaps to moral
progress in almost all religions. Through it
primitive cultures and moral customs which
happen to be enshrined in the canon become
absolutely authoritative, and the weight of
their influence is set against new ventures in
moral life.

If Calvinistic and puritan idealism departed
from its assumed norm in its very conception,
the moral realities which issued from it bore
even less resemblance to the absolute idealism
of the ethics of Jesus. Its unqualified confidence in the power of individual virtue to overcome the world and change society contributed
to the relaxation of moral restraints upon
social institutions and the secularization of
society to which reference has been made. Its

sanctification of secular tasks led inevitably to a sanctification of secular motives which it did not desire but could not prevent. Men were to serve God by diligence in their daily toil. But what was the end of industry which endowed it with virtue? The puritan answer was to regard work as an end in itself, an emphasis which it learned to make in its reaction to monastic and aristocratic idleness. But that answer alone could not suffice. Inevitably the material gains which were the rewards of industry were given a special religious sanction. "If God show you a way in which you may lawfully get more than in another way, without wrong to your soul or to any other, if you refuse this and choose the less gainful, you cross one of the ends of your Calling and refuse to be God's steward," said Governor Bradford.[2] The ancient and medieval world had been more or less scornful of the pursuit of wealth and abounded in characters among both the nobility and the peasantry who thought it beneath their dignity to increase their patri-

[2] Quoted by Tawney, *op. cit.*

mony. The religious sanction of material gain was a new thing in history and undoubtedly helped to fashion the moral temper of modern society in which diligence is the great virtue and greed the besetting vice.[3] It is the puritan heritage of America which gives a clew to the paradox of our national life. It explains how we can be at the same time the most religious and the most materialistic of all modern nations.

If puritanism failed to see how easily the virtue of thrift might be transmuted into the vice of avarice, it was even less careful to guard the righteous soul against the perils to virtue which inhere in the power which wealth supplies. There are few men who can wield extraordinary power without making it the tool of their own desires and without magnifying their limitations which might pass unnoticed in less puissant individuals. Puritanism did indeed have a doctrine of stewardship, but it was applied to the privilege which flowed from

[3] The relation of puritanism to modern capitalism has been most exhaustively treated by Max Weber in his essay on "Die Protestantische Ethic und der Geist des Kapitalismus."

economic power and not to the possession of power itself. There was never enough imagination in puritanic religion to detect how nature in the soul of man, frustrated by a discipline of the senses, comes into its own through the sins of the mind. It knew how to redeem human life from its vagrant passions, but it did not know how to deal with those dominant desires, the lust for power and the greed for gain, which express themselves more frequently in a disciplined personality than in a chaotic one and which may be more detrimental to the welfare of others than the consequences of undisciplined and momentary passions. It was a spiritual discipline admirably suited to lift the middle classes to a dominant position in society but hardly designed to guide them in the use of the power once they had achieved it. Even its abhorrence of luxury and prohibition of extravagance is finally softened in a civilization which has profited all too well by its virtues and is tempted to destroy them by the very advantages which the virtues supplied. John Wesley, who revived puritan morality after it had declined in its original form, saw this problem more clearly than his predecessors, but he had no answer for it except to advocate philanthropic generosity. He writes in his *Journal*: "Religion must necessarily produce both industry and frugality, and these cannot but produce riches. But as riches increase so will pride, anger and love of the world in all its branches. . . . So although the form of religion remains, the spirit is swiftly vanishing away. Is there no way to prevent this—this continual decay of pure religion? We ought not prevent people from being diligent and frugal; we must exhort all Christians to gain all they can and save all they can; that is, in effect, to grow rich. What way then can we take that our money may not sink us in the the nethermost hell? There is one way and there is no other under heaven. If those who gain all they can and save all they can will likewise give all they can, then the more they give the more will they grow in grace and the more treasure will they lay in heaven." ‘

‘ Quoted in Southey's *Life of Wesley*, Chapter xxix.

Wesley, of course, could hardly be expected to appreciate that money represents power even more than privilege in modern society, and that philanthropy may become a method of satisfying the ego and displaying power.

Many of the moral and religious limitations of modern civilization may be attributed first to the partial victory and then to the self-destruction of puritan religion in modern civilization. In puritanism religion made one of its boldest advances upon the world; and so confident was it of victory that it prepared no one for the moral relativities which were the inevitable issue of its enterprise. In dealing with the stubborn resistance of the material world it is better to expect victory than to assume defeat before the battle is begun. Yet an undue confidence may be as dangerous to the enterprise as a timorous spirit. The medieval ascetics who regarded all human relationships with a critical spirit, and rather expected the old Adam to assert himself in seemingly the most innocent human concerns, possessed spiritual insights which were totally lacking in the typical puritan. He expected to build a society in which the scripture was "really and materially to be fulfilled."

It will have been noted that Calvinism and puritanism have been used in this discussion as interchangeable terms. The fact is that, while the two terms are not synonymous theologically, the moral temper of Calvinism was so potent in the whole non-Lutheran Protestant world that all of the various denominations were indoctrinated with its puritan spirit. The various sects had their own theological peculiarities, but in their puritan spirit they were essentially one. Only the Quakers departed from it; for George Fox had discovered the ethics of Jesus, and the religion of the Friends was ever after to express itself in terms relevant to the spirit of the Sermon on the Mount. Denominations such as the Baptists and Methodists who evangelized Western America gave a rebirth to the puritan spirit when it suffered decay in its more native haunts. Their history is additional evidence for the thesis that puritanism is a religious sublimation of the life of the middle classes. For when the heroic spirit of puritanism declined in those classes which it had lifted to power, it was reborn in the lower middle classes of England and the Western pioneers of America. Methodism is theologically as unrelated to Calvinism as can be imagined. Its theological presuppositions are really more congenial to a dynamic puritanism than those of Calvinism; for the moral vigor of Calvinism was logically incompatible with its deterministic faith. Denominations such as the Baptists and Methodists with their strong emphasis on regeneration as the basis of church membership aggravated one weakness of Protestantism, for all of their spiritual vigor. Their tests of what constituted regeneration were drawn from religious experience rather than from its moral fruits; yet they were bound to assume that a marked moral contrast existed between the saved and the unsaved. Thus they accentuated what Professor A. Whitehead has defined as the Protestant over-simplification of ethics, i.e., a tendency to judge men, in spite of the intricacy of their inner life and the complexity of their social relations, as being either good or bad. This is simply another aspect of Protestant individualism, but it is an aspect which emerges more clearly in the free churches which have renounced all ambition to have a membership coextensive with the citizenship of the state than in those churches in which some vestige of the state-church idea still remains. The superior spiritual vigor of churches which make a religious experience the prerequisite of fellowship in the church may well be conceded; but that does not change the fact that ethical values in a complex civilization are frequently imperiled by the oversimplification of moral issues, which is the inevitable by-product of simple religious tests. Men are neither totally good nor totally bad when they live in a society which may corrupt the virtuous intention of the most robust idealist, or when their own inner life is so complex that moral purpose may express itself in one of its areas and be betrayed in another. There is a moral simplicity in Protestantism which is closely related to its individualism and which is particularly unfortunate, since it is the characteristic of a religion which orients the ethical life of peoples who have tremendous responsibilities in the complex life of Western civilization.

Calvinism has frequently been referred to as Protestant asceticism.[5] Its robust moral energies are indeed commensurate with the strict ethical discipline of medieval monasticism, but with this difference: that one is developed within the world and the other outside of the world of ordinary human relations. But it is precisely this difference which makes Lutheranism more closely related to asceticism than Calvinism; for Lutheranism is the Protestant way of despairing of the world and of claiming victory for the religious ideal without engaging the world in combat. Both are founded upon an ethical dualism. The medieval ascetic flees from the world into the monastery and there attempts realization of his religious ideal; the Lutheran quietist flees

[5] Both Max Weber and E. Troeltsch make much of the relation of Calvinism to medieval asceticism. See Max Weber, *op. cit.*, and E. Troeltsch, *Sociallehren der Christlichen Kirche.*

from the world into the asylum of his inner
life where he comes into the emotional possession of the ideal without risking its refinements in the world of cruel realities. The one
has a dualism which divides the monastic from
ordinary men; the other draws the line within
the soul of each individual and expects him to
realize in his religious experience what he cannot reveal in ordinary human relations. If
Calvinism is *Weltfreundlich,* Lutheranism like
asceticism is *Weltfeindlich.* It has little hope
that a kingdom of God will be established upon
earth, except perhaps through supernatural
intervention. It places all its emphasis upon
the sentiment of Jesus: "The kingdom of God
is within you." It must be admitted that
Jesus' conception of the kingdom of God is
probably as much related to quietistic religion
as to puritan morality, though ascetic religion
seems closer to him than either. The modern
church has dismissed the eschatological element in Jesus' teachings as the Semitic shell in
which Jesus developed his conception of the
kingdom of God as a social ideal; but it was

[111]

more probably his way of expressing doubt
that his ideal could ever be realized in history
except by a miracle of God. Yet the apoca-
lyptic element in the gospel was qualified by
the idea of the kingdom to be realized by evolutionary process. The kingdom of God was
also "like unto a mustard seed." Jesus in short
was both pessimistic and optimistic in regard
to the spiritual potentialities of human society,
and in his paradoxical rather than consistent
position he was able to maintain the tension
between religion and life in a way which has
escaped both parties in the churches of the
Reformation. Of this more will be said later.
The attitude of Lutheran piety toward the
world has the merit and the limitation characteristic of all pessimism. It sharpens the
ideal but despairs of its realization. Lutheran
doctrine was fashioned out of the religious
experiences of a tumultuous soul seeking peace
and failing to find it in any of the institutions
which were meant to incarnate the religious
ideal or in any of the observance which were
intended to express it. The institution shocked

him by their imperfections, and the observances and rituals had undergone the inevitable process which reduces a necessary symbolism to a kind of magic in which the symbol achieves potencies originally ascribed only to the ineffable truth or reality for which it stands. From all historic relativities of the institutions and superficialities of religious rites Luther reacted and discovered his absolute in the religious experience in which the soul appropriates the grace of God. In that mystic communion all natural imperfections of the human spirit are transcended and the soul is lifted out of the relativities of time and circumstance. It is easy to see how inevitable is this emphasis in the history of religion but also how perilous it may become to moral values. It is inevitable because every sensitive conscience suffers at times from a realization that "our reach is beyond our grasp," that moral capacities are not equal to the goals set by imagination and hope. The apostle Paul, whose religious experience closely paralleled those of Luther and whose theology therefore became authori-

tative for him, complained: ". . . the good
that I would, I do not; but the evil which I
would not, that I do. . . . For I delight in the
law of God after the inward man. But I see
another law in my members, warring against
the law in my mind and bringing me into cap-
tivity to the law of sin that is in my members.
O wretched man that I am. Who shall deliver
me from the body of this death? I thank God
through Jesus Christ our Lord." [o] That is a
classic statement of the dualism in life which
every religion is tempted to overcome by transcending it. Lutheranism was in fact but a
revival of Pauline Christianity and it was
Pauline Christianity which had built the Christian church. In it the tension between religion
and life which is maintained in the religious
idealism of Jesus is relaxed and the sensitive
soul is given the assurance that a merciful God
will know how to complete what is so incom-
plete and how to perfect our manifest imperfections. Thus the same Jesus who in the
gospels is a bold adventurer of the spirit who

[o] Romans vii. 19-25.

[114]

challenges his disciples to be perfect as their
Father in heaven is perfect becomes in the
epistles the symbol of the divine grace which
knows how to accept our intentions for our
achievements. It may be unfair to speak of a
conflict between the religion of Jesus and the
religion of Paul; for it was a heavenly Father
and not a jealous judge who was central in
the thought of Jesus, and his emphasis upon
forgiveness shocked the strict moralists of his
day. But if there is no conflict at this point,
there is a marked change in emphasis. In the
one the appropriation of divine grace is a
necessary part of the moral adventure; in the
other it is separated from the moral enterprise
and easily becomes a substitute for it. Paul
had indeed disavowed all antinomian tendencies in his doctrine of grace. "What shall we
then say? Shall we continue to sin that grace
may abound? God forbid. How shall we that
are dead to sin, live any longer therein?"
Obviously the mystical experience in both the
Pauline and the Lutheran religion was not
unrelated to the life of moral purpose and was

not consciously used to obviate the necessity for moral enterprise. But what is to prevent men from making a premature appropriation of the peace it guarantees, before and without deserving it? In that lies a peril to morality in almost all religion which Pauline and Lutheran theology did not create but which it may accentuate. It is well to remember that some of the greatest perils to morality in the life of religion arise out of its most cherished and necessary characteristics. Religion is at once the necessary partner and the potential foe of moral life.

The quietistic tendencies of religion, particularly as elaborated by Pauline and Lutheran theology, are less dangerous in a simple society than in a complex one. Ethical attitudes in simple social relations flow almost automatically out of a religious experience, even though the conscious interpretation of the experience is scornful of the "righteousness of works." But in the secondary and more complex social relationships the moral urge which issues out of the religious experience is easily frustrated by the intricacies and relativities of historic realities and institutions. How shall the soul preserve the sense of the absolute which it has gained in the religious experience from contamination by the sins which are covert in all social relations? It is in the varying answers of quietistic religion to that question that its ethical limitations are vividly revealed. One answer is to avoid conflict with political and social institutions on the score that they are divinely ordained. "Let every soul be subject unto the higher powers. For there is no power but of God; the powers that be are ordained of God," said the apostle Paul. When it is remembered that the reference is to the government of the Roman empire, the social conservatism implicit in this logic is obvious. It was this attitude of Paul which made it easy for Luther to bring his church into such intimate union with the various governments of Germany and to maintain an attitude bordering on subservience toward the German princes. The political conservatism of Lutheranism has since been its unvarying characteristic and has had its marked effects upon history, in no period more so than in that of the World War. State churches of any kind easily become the tools of the secular state, but Lutheran state churches have usually been more compliant tools than the Anglican church, for instance, which has never quite renounced the old Catholic ambitions of partnership with the state.

Another method of which quietistic religion avails itself in dealing with the world is to assume that its ideal will somehow achieve automatic realization in the intricacies of economic and social life. This method is hardly consistent with its pessimism, but it satisfies the desire for practical results which is bound to assert itself in even the most supra-moral religion. Thus Luther declares: [7] "There can be no better instructions in . . . all transactions in temporal goods than that every man who is to deal with his neighbor present to himself these commandments: 'What you would

[7] *Grosser Sermon vom Wucher* (*Werke,* Vol. IV, page 49).

that others should do unto you, do ye also to them,' and 'Love thy neighbor as thyself.' If these were followed out, then everything would arrange and instruct itself; all things would quietly and simply be set to rights, for everyone's heart and conscience would guide him." It is a conceit of religious people, by no means confined to Lutherans, that a vigorous statement of the ideal ought to result in its realization. No one can estimate how often the pulpit has insisted in these latter days that war could be abolished if only the nations "would live according to the law of Christ." This characteristic frequently gives the church's pronouncements a curious air of futility; for ideals are neither challenged nor applied if they are not finally embodied in concrete proposals for specific situations. It is in such situations that the ideal meets its real test and runs the peril of corruption. Frequently the tendency of religion to be content with the statement of abstract principles is due to a want of intellectual vigor which results easily from religion's mistrust of reason.

A method of dealing with the world which is more consistent with the essential dualism of quietistic religion is its effort to give some realization to the ideal by means of subjective religious emotion which transcends the imperfections of society without attempting to change them. Thus the ideal of brotherhood is to be realized by a religious appreciation of all men as brothers, however much economic and social facts may give the lie to the ideal. This was the apostle Paul's method of dealing with slavery and Luther emulated it in his attitude toward the peasant's revolt. Nothing gives a more illuminating clue to the conservative implications of this type of religion than this incident in the Reformation. The peasants, suffering in a state of semi-slavery, saw in Luther's statement of the gospel principles of freedom, and in the religious ideal of the equal worth of all souls, implicit in Christian teaching, a justification for their revolt against the intolerable conditions of serfdom. They declared: "It has been custom hitherto for men to hold us as their own property, which

is pitiable enough considering that Christ has
delivered and redeemed us all, the lowly as
well as the great, by the shedding of his
precious blood. Accordingly it is consistent
with scripture that we should be free and
should wish to be so. We therefore take it for
granted that you will release us from serfdom
as true Christians, unless it should be shown
from the gospels that we are serfs." [8] Luther
violently disavowed this practical application
of his gospel. "This article would make all
men equal and so change the spiritual kingdom
of Christ into an external worldly one. Impossible. An earthly kingdom cannot exist without inequality of persons. Some must be free,
others serfs, some rulers, others subjects. As
St. Paul says, 'In Christ there is neither bond
nor free.'" The violence of Luther's reaction
in this instance was partly due to considerations of expediency; for he feared to lose caste
with the princes by having the Reformation
identified with radical political movements; yet

[8] Article 3 in Twelve Articles, quoted by J. S. Shapiro in
Social Reform and the Reformation.

it is fairly faithful to his general conceptions of the nature and function of religion. Obviously the dualism of Protestantism which separates the religious experience of the individual from the social realities in which alone personality can achieve significance has defects which are more perilous to social values than the ethical dualism of medieval monasticism. If the ideal is to be withdrawn from life to save it from corruption, it is better that it be realized in some social medium, however artificial, than that it be suspended in the thin air of religious sentiment and be realized only in subjective experience.

An analysis of the various strategies of religion in establishing contact with the historic situations and social realities in which it must function reveals, in short, that it can pursue no course which is altogether free of peril to its moral values. Capitulation without conflict reduces religion to magic and secularizes life. A stubborn conflict with the intractable forces of nature and history results in some kind of compromise. Neither papal internationalism nor puritan plutocracy are what the idealists who were responsible for them really desired. And what they really desired fell short of their pretended goals. Withdrawal from the world is equally dangerous. For it may lead either to the morbid artificialities of asceticism or to the sentimental subjectivism of quietistic religion. There are values in each of the various strategies as well as perils. Perhaps those who are too critical of their limitations can never create their values. Religion must create its values in naïve faith and subject their limitations to a critical intelligence. Of the various strategies aceticism is probably nearest to the real genius of religion and most adequate for the moral needs of our day. If a world is completely astray the higher perspective from which it may be convicted of sin and the greater dynamic which may function redemptively in its life both depend upon some kind of detachment of religion from life.

CHAPTER VI

SOCIAL COMPLEXITY AND ETHICAL IMPOTENCE

WHILE there is good reason to regret the individualism of Protestantism in a civilization which has increased the intimacy of all human relations and made social and economic interdependence a basic fact, yet it alone cannot be held responsible for the unethical nature of modern society. This is attributable as much to the greater difficulties which the human conscience faces in modern life as to any weakness in the moral and religious idealism by which it is informed. A much more adequate type of religious idealism might have been unequal to the task of preserving ethical values in modern life.

The gradual secularization of economics through the growing complexity of commercial relations has been a previous interest of our study. When it became inconvenient and difficult to make simple moral standards, expressed in prohibitions of usury and maintenance of a "just price," fit the new intricacies of international commerce and industrial production, we have seen how men turned naturally and inevitably to the consoling reflection that "in the providence of God life is so arranged that each man seeking his own shall serve the common weal." The doctrine of laissez faire was in other words as much an admission of defeat on the part of the moral forces of society as it was a conscious effort toward secularization. Other factors beside a growing complexity of social life helped however to secularize modern society. Modern commerce and industry tend to increase the extent of coöperative effort while they diminish personal contacts. World commerce and large-scale production make human beings interdependent without offering them the opportunity of entering upon personal associations. There is a natural sympathy in the soul which saves men from actions which are very obviously detrimental to their fellows. But if they are unable to survey the consequences of their actions or to gauge the reactions to their attitudes in the lives of others, their temptation to unethical conduct is materially increased. The master of a manufacturing unit in the old handcraft period of industry thus found it much easier to maintain moral relations to his workers than a modern, frequently absentee, owner of a large factory. If in addition ownership becomes collective, with the resulting division of responsibility, while the number of workers increases until individuals lose their significance in the mass, the problem of making industrial relations ethical is further complicated. Ethical conduct is, in its last analysis, based upon reverence for personality; and personality fails to make its appeal to the conscience when considered in the mass and when regarded at too long range. In such circumstances a degree of intelligence and imagination, which mankind has not yet achieved, is required to gauge the effect of industrial and commercial policy upon the individuals who are involved in it. The unethical nature of modern civilization with its destruction of confidence in the moral integrity of human nature and with its deterministic obsessions is largely due to its mechanical perfections which have increased the extent of social coöperation while they have decreased personal contacts.

The same means of commerce and communication which have increased the size of industrial groups and extended the range of commercial transactions have also enlarged the political units and increased interdependence between them. We are living in a world in which a financial depression in America results in a panic upon the silk exchange of Tokio; in which a boycott upon cotton goods initiated by a Gandhi in India throws thousands of cotton spinners in Manchester into unemployment; and in which Western industrialism may exploit Chinese labor in the seaports of China without one beneficiary of this industrialism out of a million being able to make a mental picture of the social consequences of the commercial policies from which he benefits. The difficulty of these long-range relationships is further complicated by the fact that the participants are separated not only by great distances but by the barriers of race and nationality. All social decencies in the past have developed within the bounds of the group, and men have not yet learned to treat individuals in other groups with confidence, respect and honesty. Attitudes of tenderness, sympathy and affection have been confined very largely to the family group. From this intimate group they were finally sluiced out to effect social relations in larger groups, but they have not changed inter-group relations. Civilization has increased the size of groups in which human relations have an ethical basis, but it has not moralized the action of the group nor taught individuals in one social group to treat individuals in other groups with the respect and confidence which a wholesome social life requires. The connotation of contempt which the Jews placed in the word "gentile" and the Greeks in the word "barbarian" may be matched in the terminology of practically every people. When groups are geographically separated, as

in the case of political states, fear and misunderstanding are multiplied by the ignorance
which results from a lack of contacts. But
contacts alone do not remove them; for the
relations of political, social and racial groups
within the boundaries of the same state are only
slightly more ethical, as for instance the relation between white and colored people in the
United States or of the Scotch and Irish in
Ulster. Human imagination and intelligence
have not been equal to the task of extending
ethical attitudes beyond the boundaries of the
group.

The ethical problem of group relations is
made still more difficult by the expansive
desires and unethical attitudes which develop
naturally within the group as a corporate
entity. That is, groups as such find it even
more difficult to maintain moral attitudes
toward other groups than do the individuals
within it toward individuals in other racial or
political unities. All human groups tend to be
more predatory than the individuals which
compose them. The most tender emotions may

characterize the relations of members of a family to each other; but the family as such is easily tempted to gain its advantages at the expense of other families. The tendency of family loyalty to accentuate covetousness has been frequently noted by social observers who have seen the family instinct as the very basis of the sanctity which civilization has given private property. Religious organizations are not free of the imperial ambitions which come naturally to social groups of every kind. One fruitful cause of the dilution of religious idealism is the desire of religious groups to gain power and prestige among larger numbers. They therefore soften the rigor of their ideal that it may captivate the morally mediocre majority. Both employers and employees frequently find agreement in specific cases of conflict difficult because the policies of both are determined by considerations of loyalty to their respective groups. Of all human groups the political state is probably most inclined to unethical conduct. It was a dictum of George Washington's that a nation was not to be trusted beyond its interests, and history supports the justice of his observation. After shrewdly observing the statesmen of England equivocate on the attitude of their nation toward the southern rebellion until they could determine their policy by considerations of expediency, Henry Adams came to the melancholy conclusion that masses of men were always moved by interest and never by conscience and that morality is a private and a costly luxury.[1] One reason why the relations of nations to each other are still characterized by primitive fears and excessive caution is because their actions have not, as a matter of fact, been morally dependable. The problem of making nations and other groups conform to ethical standards of any kind is particularly difficult because the ethical attitude of the individual toward his group easily obscures the unethical nature of the group's desires. The patriot identifies his tender emotions toward his nation with the attitude of the nation itself until he becomes incapable of a critical

[1] In his *Education of Henry Adams,* Chapter x.

appraisal of its policy; or he frankly condones the selfishness of the nation because he recognizes no ethical values beyond those implicit in group loyalty. The father of a family may feel moral pride in essentially selfish pursuits because he means to secure advantages by them not for himself but for his family. Loyalty to "the firm" may give the business man a consciousness of virtue even though it forces him to connive in predatory practices of his concern. The class-conscious worker may be willing to disrupt society in the interest of his class because all his moral needs are satisfied by his devotion to what he regards as the most significant social group. While this ethical paradox of patriotism is obviously not confined to political groups, the nation is most seriously tempted to unethical conduct because it is not a voluntary association, its group is conveniently isolated from others and loyalty to it is least qualified by other conflicting loyalties. It may be set down as a truth of almost axiomatic finality, that groups tend to be unethical in proportion to the degree of unqualified loyalty which they are able to claim or exact of their members. In this connection it may be noted that democracy has increased rather than diminished the imperialism of nations, for it has given patriotism a higher moral sanction and thus reduced the moral scruples which might qualify the loyalty of their citizens. The arrogance of nations and their insistence on moral autonomy has developed simultaneously with the extension of democracy. It is this ethical paradox of patriotism which invalidates the contention that the root of all imperialism is the imperialism of the individual. It is true of course that group loyalty may become a device for delegating our vices to the group and imagining ourselves virtuous. Some types of political arrogance and race prejudice are obviously methods of compensating individuals for their lack of opportunity to bully their immediate neighbors. Yet on the whole the unethical character of group action is determined as much by the partial virtues as by the vices of individuals.

The problem of bringing groups under some kind of ethical control is not new in history. It has become unusually difficult in the modern world not only because of the consolidation of the authority of the state but also because rapid means of communication have increased the size of social, political and economic units and made relations between them more intricate. The larger the unit the more unqualified seems to be the moral sanction which loyalty to it may claim. To an average citizen, immersed in his parochial interests, the nation appears in the light of a universal community in contrast to the smaller and voluntary communities within the nation. Yet this same nation is one of many human groups, most of which betray imperial desires reminiscent of Rome but which aspire in vain after the universal dominion which gave Roman imperialism a measure of moral worth. Treitschke, whose philosophy of history was the object of so much opprobrium during the World War that its faithfulness to the general prejudices of Western life would hardly be surmised, presented the nation as the ultimate community because all smaller societies are too petty to deserve and all larger ones too vague and abstract to claim the unqualified allegiance of men.

The intricacies and propinquities of an industrial civilization tend at some points to increase the imperial desires of nations and at others to make their ordinary lusts more deadly. The feud between Germany and France is a very ancient one, but the need of French industry for German coal and of German industry for French iron explains some aspects of their present difficulties which are not derived from ancient animosities. Modern industry needs a unified world and, lacking it, each nation is inclined to seek the completion of its industrial establishment by the forcible appropriation of territory, rich in needed resources. The economic imperialism of industrially advanced nations is a product of the high productivity of modern industry which produces more than one national unit can consume and which needs more raw materials than the same nation can produce. Covetous eyes are consequently turned upon undeveloped portions of the globe, rich in raw materials and hungry for the products of modern industry. In one sense the European war was incubated in Africa. Rapid means of communication also extend the reach of the grasping nations. China is attempting to throw off the shackles of a Western imperialism which could never have gained the position it holds on Chinese soil but for the new contiguity which has destroyed the boundaries between East and West. Moreover, the intricacies of international commerce and finance offer opportunities for a new kind of economic imperialism which hardly needs, though it does not always avoid, the use of political force. The economic forces of one nation simply penetrate the economic life of another and, if there is a great disparity in economic power, the weaker nation is brought under the dominion of the stronger without the citizens of either being aware of the process by which this has been accomplished. This is the type

[136]

of imperialism which America is most fitted and inclined to develop. In South America political pressure does accompany economic penetration, but in Europe American power increases under a policy of political isolation. The isolationism of America, which has become a firmly established foreign policy since the war, is prompted partly by the sense of power which America feels as the richest nation of the world, and partly by a political infantilism which tempts us both to pharisaism and to fear when dealing with the supposedly more astute political bargainers of Europe. The relation of America to the rest of the world is a perfect example of the moral peril in the new intricacies of modern civilization. The citizen of the state is as ignorant of the actual character of his nation's relation to other nations as of other peoples' reactions to the real policy of his own government. Probably not one American in a thousand is able to comprehend a single reason why Europe should fear or hate America and not more than one in a hundred is actually aware of the existence of such hatreds and fears. There is therefore an unconscious hypocrisy in the moral pretensions of the citizens of every nation, a more or less conscious hypocrisy in the attitudes of the governments which do not share but yet exploit the political ignorance of the people, and an inevitable reaction of cynicism on the part of those who know the real facts and suffer from the moral limitations of the nation's policy. Group relations, particularly those which are intricate, are thus persistently unethical because part of the modern world is too ignorant to make them ethical and the other part is so worldly-wise that it has lost confidence in the possibility of ethical relations. Frequently hypocrisy and cynicism are united in the same person who knows how to discount the moral pretensions of other groups but lacks the perspective from which he might arrive at a critical evaluation of the real character of his own group. This curious combination of insincerity and cynicism is obvious in the relation of both economic and national groups, but it is particularly noticeable in international difficulties. In the struggle between economic groups there is a growing inclination to make no moral pretensions on either side. Sometimes the group in power makes them but in that case its insincerity is usually conscious rather than ignorant. In international affairs the same patriots who ignorantly persecute every person who seeks to qualify national loyalty or to make a dispassionate appraisal of national policies frequently sink into moral despair and disillusionment when history unfolds the inevitable consequences of the anarchy of conflicting national lusts.

The task of making complex group relations ethical belongs primarily to religion and education because statecraft cannot rise above the universal limitations of human imagination and intelligence. A robust ethical idealism, an extraordinary spiritual insight and a high degree of intelligence are equally necessary for such a social task. The difficulties of the problem are enhanced by the fact that the religious imagination and astute intelligence which are equally necessary for its solution are incom-

patible with each other. Religion is naturally
jealous of any partner in a redemptive enterprise; and the same intelligence which is needed
to guide moral purpose in a complex situation
easily lames the moral will and dulls the
spiritual insight. It is possible that this difficulty may permanently destroy every vestige
of morality in the group relations of modern
society. The necessary partnership and the
inevitable conflict between the religio-moral
and the rational forces is obvious in both the
political and the economic problems of the
present age.

The unqualified authority and the boundless
lusts of a modern state need first of all to be
brought under the scrutiny of clear minds who
understand the implications and can gauge the
consequences of its pretensions. Patriotism is
a form of altruism and as such represents the
victory of ultra-rational sanctions over the selfish inclinations of individuals which seem quite
reasonable to the average man. The emotional
attitude and ethical achievement in patriotism
endows the patriot with a kind of madness and

pride which make him as scornful of more rational types of altruism as of the prudent and cautious selfishness with which he has his primary conflict. It is because patriotism represents a victory of an ethical ideal that religion so easily becomes its uncritical partner. When many hearts are cold anything that warms them will seem religious to the undiscriminating champion of religious values. The defects of patriotic altruism are thus left to the correction of rationalistic idealists who know how to discover the absurdities into which an uncritical devotion to partial values may issue and how to envisage the larger community of mankind of which the nation is a part. During the last war moral idealists of rationalistic persuasion, such as Bertrand Russell, Romain Rolland, Henri Barbusse and Bernard Shaw, were more detached in their perspective and freer of war hysterias than any religious leaders of equal standing. To envisage the larger community of mankind which lacks the physical symbols of the state and to dispel the parochial prejudices which are harbored in mediocre minds and which make hatred of others the inevitable commitant of love for one's own is clearly a task to which a discriminating intelligence must contribute.

However the problem of group relations, as has been previously noted, is created not only by the parochialism of individuals but by the lust and greed of the group itself. The task of persuading the group to sacrifice some of its advantages for the sake of the whole of human society is so difficult that it almost leads to despair. If it will ever be accomplished religio-moral forces, whatever their present impotence, must come to the aid of reason. Prudence alone may prompt nations to a measure of self-sacrificing action, since unqualified self-assertion must lead to mutual destruction. But prudential morality reveals the same defects in intergroup relations which we have noted in simpler social problems. Its ends are always too immediate and its perspective is too narrow. Moral action which lacks some reference to an absolute standard and some ultra-rational dynamic inevitably falls short even of satisfy-

ing the social necessities. The prudence· of
nations in the present state of international
relations tends to prompt a few, usually neigh-
boring nations, to compose their differences, but
for the sake and at the price of sharpening the
conflict with some other alliance of states. The
net result of such an enterprise is simply to
enlarge the unit of conflict once more without
abolishing warfare. The manner in which the
triple entente and the triple alliance, both
formed with high moral pretensions, helped to
make the World War inevitable is a matter of
history. More recently there are indications
that France and Germany will compose their
differences "for the sake of Europe." Such
a reconciliation will hasten the unification of
Europe but will also help to raise the specter
of intercontinental wars with continental units
of conflict. The unification of Asia upon a
basis of common resentment against Western
imperialism is an almost unavoidable development in international affairs. All these continental alliances are logical enough from any
immediate perspective but dangerous from the

perspective of the welfare of the whole race. There is no indication that prudential state-craft has the resources to prevent America from inciting the whole of Europe against our economic overlordship of that continent. The increasing feeling aroused by the problem of debt liquidations is symptomatic of the natural resentment which must inevitably issue out of a relation of economic interdependence between a very wealthy and a poor continent. For the settlement of this issue no policy will be wise except one which will appear very foolish to the wise statesmen. A prudent statecraft has made the anxiety of a wealthy creditor the dominant note in American international policy, and envy and fear the chief character-istics in the attitudes of the peoples who must deal with us.

Social intelligence does of course produce a finer fruit than the type of prudence which char-acterizes the international policy of modern states. There is a whole class of social idealists who understand the economic basis of most international difficulties and who would bring peace to the warring classes and nations by an economic reorganization of modern society. Since modern industrialism and capitalism have materially complicated the ancient feuds between races and classes, it is evident that no amount of moral and spiritual goodwill can produce an ordered and stable international society if the economic roots of war are not clearly discerned and finally eliminated. However the same intelligence which is capable of such discernment easily drifts into a cynicism which discounts all moral and personal factors in social reconstruction and places its hope entirely in a new social strategy. Loyalty to the class is substituted for loyalty to the state, and class conflict is expected to issue in a lasting peace for both classes and nations. Economic determinists show a superior discernment in recognizing that in a civilization which is forced to organize its economic life across national boundaries the conflict of interest between classes does become more significant than the conflict between states, particularly since the latter conflict is due either to economic or to fantastic and imaginary causes. But their very realism betrays them into a cynicism which finally issues in the most romantic and unrealistic dreams. They imagine that social peace will result from the victory of one class over all other classes. They have not taken into account that modern capitalism produces a formidable middle class the interests of which are not identical with the proletarians. Moral and spiritual considerations may conceivably prompt this class to make common cause with the workers in the attainment of ethical social ends, but it will never be annihilated even by the most ruthless class conflict nor will it be persuaded by the logic of economic facts that its interests are altogether identical with those of the workers. Even if one class were able to eliminate all other classes, which is hardly probable, it would require some social grace and moral dynamic to preserve harmony between the various national groups by which this vast mass would be organized and into which it would disintegrate. Even within one national unit any economic class will dissolve into various groups, according to varying and sometimes conflicting interests, as soon as its foes are eliminated. The Russian communists were not long able to preserve their absolute solidarity after their revolution was firmly established. The dominant group soon learned that no amount of ruthlessness was able to prevent the gradual formation of a minority group under Trotzky and Zinoviev. Significantly, the conflict of interest between peasants and industrial workers is the real basis of this schism within communist ranks.

In Europe the qualification of patriotism by class loyalties has in some instances led to a mitigation of national animosities, but it has not destroyed them. On the contrary it has added new hatreds to the old and created a society which is divided not only by vertical but also by horizontal divisions. The Marxian idea of the unification of the world upon the basis of the common interests of the proletarian class must be relegated to the category of millenial dreams. It is based upon an illusion little better than that of nationalism.

The nationalists seek to escape the moral problem by delegating the vices of the individual to the group and the Marxians fantastically endow the group with virtues which it does not possess. Religious and moral idealism, preaching goodwill and peace without taking the brutal realities of the modern economic conflict into consideration, is little better, and probably less serviceable than a cynical realism which is blind to everything but the secular facts revealed in modern economic life. The moral futility of such idealism is one of the very roots of such a cynicism. Yet, finally, the problem of social reconstruction cannot be solved without the resources of religious insight and moral goodwill. The economic reorganization of society will not be effected without conflict between those who possess the privileges and those who suffer from the inequalities of modern industrialism. Neither can it be effected without the mutual sacrifice of rights, the mutual forgiveness of sins and a mutual trust going beyond the deserts of any party to the controversy. In England, where economic theory and practice has never been as completely divorced from religious idealism as on the Continent, a gradual transfer political power and social privilege to the ranks of the workers is being made with much less peril of a social convulsion than in any nation of the Continent. Both the possessors of privilege and those who challenge the possession are stubborn in the defense of their advantages and in the championship of their rights; but at least a measure of influence upon the struggle is exercised by spiritual and moral considerations which Continental critics of England identify with the British capacity for compromise but which probably has deeper and more spiritual roots. Meanwhile religious idealism in America is almost completely corrupted by sentimentality and betrayed into social futility because the momentary unification of American society upon the basis of the interests of the middle classes absolves the religious conscience from facing the moral challenge in the social and economic facts of modern society.

Economic determinists are not alone in

sharing with an ordinary prudential statecraft in the effort to organize the life of groups by means of the resources of intelligence. The hopes of the more conventional yet socially intelligent people for a new world are involved in the idea of a society or league of nations. Since an inchoate international society created by the new intimacy in which nations live exists in spite of international anarchy, it is reasonable to attempt the creation of more adequate forms and machinery for the crystallization and expression of its collective will, the conciliation of disputes among its members and the closer integration of its life. Moral and spiritual forces are sometimes frustrated merely by the lack of adequate machinery for the application of generally accepted principles to specific situations. There is therefore great need for an intelligent statesmanship which will give the soul of an international society a body, and incarnate its aspirations in the instruments of political order.

From another point of view, however, international society does not yet exist and needs to be created; and the means for its creation are not laws but attitudes, not organization but a type of life. Politically minded people easily suffer from the illusion that laws create morality, that organization creates society. Societies are not created by political mechanism but by attitudes of mutual respect and trust. Where these exist social relations are established and traditions formed. These in turn are gradually codified and given definition and precision by legal enactments. No one now takes the theory seriously that human society was created by a conscious mutual contract between individuals who suddenly realized that they could save themselves in no other way from mutual self-destruction. Society is older than human history and exists wherever individuals establish relations of mutual reverence and trust. The family is usually the beginning of society because here nature aids the imagination and consanguinity creates an atmosphere of mutual trust. The family is enlarged by the fortunes and the needs of war, the resulting clans may amalgamate into larger units

through intermarriage of leaders or through
other exigencies, and the emerging national or
racial group is formed by similar forces. The
love and trust which unite a society are no
more rational than the hatred and mistrust
which divide one society from another. People
do not regard each other as morally dependable because reason persuades or experience
prompts them to such an attitude. The attitude is determined by natural and instinctive
or by ideal and religious forces and, once it is
assumed, is inevitably verified; for in an atmosphere of mutual trust human action finally
becomes trustworthy and morally dependable.
In so far as national and racial groups live
in a state of mutual fear and hold life outside
of the group in contempt rather than in reverence there is no international society nor can
political machinery create it. Only in rare
instances are new social traditions created by
legal enactments. Political forms and legal
measures are usually belated recognitions of
previously established social facts and necessities. The problem of group relations in mod-

ern society is as difficult as it is because natural causes have operated to make the social units larger and larger while no ideal forces have been strong enough to prompt the group to enter into ethical relations with other groups. If a higher degree of imagination than now seems probable does not inform the life of modern nations only, one further step is possible—the consolidation of continents. In such an eventuality the present League of Nations could easily become the instrument of pan-Europeanism in conflict with other Continents. A society of nations is impossible, in short, without those ultra-rational attitudes which either instinct or religion must create and which in the case of this final venture is beyond the resources of natural instincts—except in the event of a threat from some other planetary community.

If the creation of an international society is a task to which moral and spiritual resources must contribute, its maintenance and development are no less dependent upon the coöperation of spiritual insight with political prudence.

Even at best human nature is so imperfect and relations between groups as well as individuals so fruitful in misunderstandings that it is impossible to maintain the mutual trust and confidence which are the basis of society without the spiritual achievement of mutual repentance and forgiveness. In the relation between groups the ability to detect flaws in one's own and extenuating circumstances in the actions and attitudes of others is at once more necessary and more difficult than in intra-group relations. It is more difficult because the intricacy and long range of the relations, and the inevitable hypocrisy in the pretensions of governments, easily obscure the limitations of one and the virtues and good intentions of the other party of the relationship. It is more necessary because the frictions which fret the relations of national and other groups are much more generally due to mutual guilt than those of individual relations. They develop in a narrow world and in a society of but few members in which a suspected peril may lead to a gesture of defense, the defensive measure

[154]

be regarded as offensive and in turn prompt an actual attack which will be justified in turn as a defensive measure. Thus fears produce hatreds, hatreds express themselves in ugly grimaces and someone finally strikes the first blow. The World War resulted from a spontaneous combustion of fears and hatreds, and the partial mobilizations, full mobilizations and final declarations of war are so intimately related to each other that impartial historians find it increasingly difficult and irrelevant to decide who was responsible for the actual hostilities. The obvious fact is that every generation of every European state for several centuries had gathered fuel for flames of war. Yet each group declared its absolute innocence and heaped abuse upon the foe. Years after the conflict only a small minority in each of the participating nations has had the imagination to see or the grace to confess the share of its nation in the mutual guilt. Meanwhile ancient feuds are perpetuated because the hypocrisy of the victors is written into solemn treaties and produces a resentment among the vanquished which makes them incapable of any higher sincerity. Issues between nations are so involved that only expert knowledge is able to ascertain the real facts, but the very intricacies of the problems involved make it possible to use the facts for the validation of almost any thesis which national pride may dictate. The real task of persuading groups to encourage forgiveness by repentance and repentance by forgiveness, and thus to overcome rather than perpetuate evil, is a spiritual and a moral one and cannot be accomplished in a completely secular atmosphere. There is little evidence to justify the hope that spiritual and moral forces, as they are now oriented, are prepared to aid in such a task. But their responsibility is obvious; social intelligence may be a partner in the process of conciliation but intelligence cannot bear the burden alone when a disposition to humility and a capacity for mercy is lacking.

Urging the necessity of religious attitudes between social and political groups may seem to be a counsel of perfection when it is remem-

bered that intra-group relations, except in the
circle of the family and in small religious fel-
lowships, have never been able to profit by their
aid. Society in general has usually contented
itself with the expedient of composing social
friction and arbitrating dispute by apportion-
ing the relative guilt and innocence of the disputants through a presumably impartial
judicatory which enforces its decisions upon
the belligerents, however irreconcilable or
obstreperous they may be. But the fact is that
such a method is both easier and more effective
in a society composed of individuals than in a
society of groups. In an ordinary national
society the impartiality of the court is guaranteed by a society of thousands and even
millions of individuals who are supposed not
to be biased in favor of one or the other litigants; and the parties to a controversy are
therefore more inclined to accept the verdict
of a court. Furthermore the society which supports the judicial tribunal is so powerful com-
pared to whatever political or physical strength
the litigants possess that it is able to enforce

the awards of the latter however recalcitrant
the disputants may be. But the society of
nations is too small, judged by the number of
its member nations, to function with absolute
impartiality in any major dispute. Judicial
action is therefore immediately less effective.
It is to be noted that courts are less serviceable
instruments of social conciliation even within
nations when they deal with large economic
and social groups such as unions and trusts or
when the issue involves basic economic problems; and the reason for this is that the parties
to a litigation represent so large a part of the
total community that the unbiased character
of the court is not as readily assumed and ought
not be taken for granted. Tradition and social
custom usually bias the court in favor of one
or the other litigants, generally the one most
firmly established in the traditional organization of the society. In the case of nations it is
obvious that for some time to come an international court must confine itself mainly to
petty disputes among powerful nations and to
the real disputes of the petty nations, from

whose perspective the large nations may represent an impartial international society.[2] Even at best no formal conciliation can heal wounds such as were made by the World War if nations cannot develop the capacity for repentance and mercy and learn how to restrain both the proud and the vindictive passions which are the natural products of unreflective social life.

Though morally dependable action develops most readily in an atmosphere of mutual trust, it is not to be assumed that either nations or individuals always justify trust by trustworthy

[2] Commenting on the first Hague conference Count Holstein of the German foreign office made some realistic observations which may not have justified his obstructive conclusions but which are nevertheless pertinent. He wrote: "Subjects of international law are states and not individuals. It will therefore be formally difficult and practically impossible to isolate the individual judge from the passions and interests of the whole in a way that happens or is supposed to happen in private law. Of all conceivable judges Great Powers are least disinterested, for in every conceivable question of any importance that may come up all Great Powers are interested à un degre quelconque. An impartial decision is therefore excluded by the nature of things. . . . Small disinterested states as subjects, small questions as objects of arbitral decision are conceivable; great states and great questions are not." (Quoted by Dickinson in *International Anarchy*, p. 351.)

action. Faith does not produce conscience automatically. Much of the pacifism now cultivated by socially effective religious forces has the defect that it fails to gauge the stubborn resistance to ideal forces in the predatory nature of national groups. It is difficult to develop moral attitudes sufficiently honest not only to give the bearer of trust the prestige of sincerity but to make the object of trust worthy of its faith. Trust united with selfishness results in moral futility; and when it is based upon illusion and fails to take account of the imperfect social attitudes which it must overcome, it issues in mere sentimentality. It is significant that the idea of the outlawry of war should be espoused particularly in America and find little favor in other nations; for here extraordinary power is united with remarkable political naïvete, so that American idealists find it difficult to appreciate the unsatisfied hungers of other nations or their resentful reaction to our own satiety. If nations cannot be moved to make some sacrifices for the sake of the ideal and to qualify their expansive desires by moral purpose, all efforts to create an international society must finally prove vain. It may be that the secular ambitions of nations are so firmly established in social custom and their unethical attitudes so generally sanctioned by the popular mind that nothing will avail to give their actions even a touch of ethical character. It is difficult enough to subdue and discipline the immediate and anarchic desires which struggle for expression in the soul of the individual; but when they express themselves in the life of groups and are veiled in seeming sanctities even while they achieve new and more diabolical forms they can be subdued only by the most astute intelligence united with a high moral passion. Modern civilization lacks both this intelligence and this moral passion and is in the peril of losing what it has of the latter as it develops the former. Moral idealism which fails to gauge the measure of resistance which its ideals must meet in the confused realities of life or to fashion adequate weapons for its conflict degenerates into mere sentimentality.

But a social intelligence which is overwhelmed by the discouraging realities and despairs of the attainment of any ideal sinks into a morally enervating cynicism. Moral leadership in Western society is divided to-day between sentimentalists and cynics who combine to render the prospect of an ethical regeneration of modern life well-nigh hopeless. If men are really to be redeemed from the sins of greed and mutual fears and hatreds by which they make their common life intolerable they need a faith which is not held too cheaply but which is held nevertheless in defiance of every discouragement. The same intelligence which the complexities of modern life demand and create easily prompts not only to the cynicism which declares that "all men are liars" but to a moral ennui which cries, "Vanity, vanity, all is vanity."

Benjamin Kidd who understood the need for ultra-rational sanctions in social life better than most sociologists put the problem of modern society in these words: "The great problem with which every progressive society stands confronted is: How to retain the highest operative ultra-rational sanctions for those onerous conditions of life which are essential to its life, and at one and the same time to allow freest play to those intellectual forces which, while tending to come into conflict with such sanctions, contribute nevertheless to raise to the highest degree of social efficiency the whole of its members." [2]

To develop the wisdom of serpents while they retain the guilelessness of doves is the task which faces the religio-moral forces if they would aid in the moral regeneration of society. It may be that such a task is too difficult for the resources of this or any generation of the immediate future and that painful experience must first prove other strategies inadequate. Meanwhile even the possibility of future usefulness of religion demands the largest possible measure of immediate detachment from the unethical characteristics of modern society. If religion cannot transform society, it must find its social function in criticizing present

[2] *Social Evolution,* page 140.

realities from some ideal perspective and in presenting the ideal without corruption, so that it may sharpen the conscience and strengthen the faith of each generation.

arises out of the nature and constitution of religion as such.

Religion in its unspoiled form is always other-worldly and disenchanted. Puritanism, romanticism and evolutionary optimism are really but reflections and refractions of the general temper of Western life, which has slowly gained the ascendancy over the religious spirit. It is a temper of friendliness to, or at least fearlessness before the world. In puritanism the tension between religion and life is maintained, but the soul is persuaded that it can bring the whole of life under the dominion of conscience. In romanticism there is a frank identification of human virtue with a sentimentally idealized natural world. Religious and ethical thought which has come under the influence of evolutionary optimism maintains a sense of tension between the soul and the natural world in rare instances; more frequently it regards human history as but the last chapter in the beautiful story of progress which all life has unfolded and which time and patience will inevitably bring to a happy issue. The foundation for the Western strategy of life was laid by the Greeks who, overcoming the awe and reverence with which the Oriental brooded over nature's mysteries, thrust impious hands into her secrets and made shrewd guesses about her varied phenomena. The Greeks learned to make only slight practical application of their knowledge, and the rise of Christianity eclipsed their scientific temper. It came into its own again at the close of the Middle Ages and at the dawn of the modern era. The fact that science developed in the West rather than the East is due to this attitude toward the natural world. The Orient is not less curious than the Occident, but it directs its mind to other problems. While it cradles philosophies and religions the West gives birth to science.

Since the dawn of the industrial era scientific knowledge is used increasingly for the purpose of transforming the natural circumstance of human life. Nature is not transcended but transformed in the interest of human happiness. Comforts are multiplied; power is increased; time and distance are destroyed;

hours of toil are reduced; natural environment
is changed; disease is eliminated and death
postponed; the hostilities of nature are overcome and her benevolence multiplied for the
sake of human welfare. Our birth may be
"but a sleep and a forgetting" but our life is
undeniably lived in natural conditions which
profoundly affect not only physical well-being
but cultural and spiritual character. It is evident therefore that there is profound wisdom
in the scientific strategy which transforms the
natural world in the interest of the human
spirit. Not only is the Western world firmly
committed to it, but there are indications that
the Orient will adopt it in spite of the opposition of religious leaders such as Gandhi. Whatever perils to the spiritual life may lurk in the
preoccupation of the soul with its physical circumstances, it is clear that human personality
may be served by improving the natural
environment which conditions it. Wealth may
lead to sensual excess but it is also the basis of
culture. Leisure may be secured by reducing
physical wants to a minimum, but there are

cultural advantages in a leisure which does not preclude the satisfaction of all reasonable desires. Comforts may lead men to become obsessed with their external circumstances, but they also reduce irrelevant distractions to life's main purpose. Physical health is not a necessary but a convenient condition for moral and spiritual enterprise.

In spite of these advantages religion, except in a few contemporary forms, has always been either hostile or indifferent to the business of transforming nature in the interest of personal values. It has counseled the soul to seek its happiness not in changing but in becoming independent of circumstances. In Buddhism the highest happiness is sought by throttling all desires. Jesus was more careful to distinguish between the will to live and its physical expressions. But he was critical of all physical desires and satisfactions. He had the Orient's profound indifference to the "business of earth." If our ears were not so habituated to his words that they fail to catch their real significance, a modern congregation would be shocked by the admonition: "Take no thought for your life, what ye shall eat or what ye shall drink; nor yet for your body, what ye shall put on. Is not life more than meat and the body more than raiment?" "Lay not up for yourselves treasures upon earth where moth and rust doth corrupt and where thieves break through and steal, for where your treasure is, there will your heart be also." "Fear not them which kill the body but are not able to kill the soul; but rather fear him which is able to destroy both soul and body in hell." The modern Christian is inclined to destroy the force of the profound other-worldliness of such sentiments by reflecting that they represent an Oriental cast which is incidental and not essential to the gospel of Jesus. They are Oriental no doubt, but precisely because they are religious; and to regard them as incidental is to miss the whole meaning of the gospel. Though the West is unable to accept them, it pays an unconscious tribute to the truth involved in them. For the absolute moral values incarnated in the personality of Jesus, which the West still reveres, are organically related to this other-worldliness.

Whatever the limitations of this emphasis, it is evident that religion cannot escape it. Concerned with the soul's inner peace and perfect virtue it is forced to lift it above the corruptions and irrelevancies of temporal conditions. The whole course of modern history is ample justification for Jesus' warning: Where your treasure is, there will your heart be also. The instruments of personality's victory over nature have become the chains for a new kind of thraldom. Western civilization is enslaved to its machines and the things which the machines produce. Spiritual forces are emancipated from the forces of nature only to become the victims of a mechanized civilization. It is a Pyrrhic victory. America, which has developed the Western strategy with greater consistency than any other nation, is at once the envy and the scorn of the world. The scorn may be a device for hiding the envy, but there is moral justification for reproach. What the world regards as our vulgarity is more than the awkwardness of youth; it is an undue pre-occupation with life's instrumentality and an obsession of the soul with the concrete world.

The Orient may be more cruel than the West, but our superior tenderness is matched by our more expansive avarice. Having determined that life consists in things a man possesses, the West sacrifices both inner peace and social harmony in the mad scramble for the power and privilege which the conquests of nature has supplied. Neither the imperialism of nations nor the monstrous avarice of economic groups is confined to Western life, but covetousness and greed have been manifestly increased by the temper and strategy of the Occident. The Biblical analysis which discovers covetousness as the root of conflict is applicable to our own day: "Ye lust and have not; ye kill and desire to have, and cannot obtain; ye fight and war, yet ye have not because ye ask amiss. . . . Know ye not that the friendship of this world is enmity with God?" [1] However necessary it may be to make

[1] James iv. 2-4.

a more equitable distribution of the physical blessings of life, religion's true function is to develop an attitude of indifference toward the very goods for the possession of which men contend so frantically. When Jesus rebuked the young man who desired his aid in correcting the inequitable division of an inheritance, his unwillingness to assume a judicial function was manifestly dictated by the thought that the whole inheritance ought to have been a matter of indifference to the young man. It is easy to see that such an attitude may lend itself to abuse and be used to perpetuate inequalities. If advocated by religious groups which have profited by economic inequalities, it becomes the tool of hypocrisy. Yet it is an emphasis which religion cannot disavow. It is basic to its whole world view.

The peril to happiness as well as to virtue in reliance upon the external fortunes of life justifies the counsel of religion that happiness must be founded on internal rather than external resources. The conquest of nature is really but a relative victory of personality over

[174]

circumstance. Though the caprice of nature's forces has been checked, fortune remains fickle. If men cannot learn "how to be abased and how to abound," there is no guarantee of happiness for them. Poverty may be a curse, but voluntarily chosen or consented to without sullenness it may become the way of the soul's emancipation. The elimination of disease is a boon to mankind, but there is little likelihood that science will be able to overcome all ills to which the human flesh is heir. No scientific advance will obviate the necessity for the discovery of faith that "God's strength is made perfect in weakness," that the infirmities of the flesh may become the occasion for the cultivation of spiritual graces. Even at best science cannot destroy nature's final irrelevancy— death. There can therefore be no real victory over nature except by the strategy of transcending her fortunes. The more hostages taken from her the greater will be the disappointment in the hour of her final victory. It is man's sublime and tragic fate that he must find happiness in the search for infinitude amidst the flux of time and he can therefore never accept the portion of mortality for himself with equanimity. Hence his final comfort must come from the counsel of religion which teaches him how he may identify himself with the eternal values of his devotion, so that "though the outward man perish yet the inward man is renewed day by day." [2]

The temper of Western civilization has made the modern church quite ashamed of the other-worldly character of traditional religion, and intent upon discarding it as much as possible. Everything is done to impress the generation with the mundane interests of religious idealism and to secularize religion itself so that it may survive in a secular age as a kind of harmless adornment of the moral life. Yet its service to both human happiness and virtue are involved in its other-worldliness. It is through that element that it gains the power to raise morality above the utilitarian plane and to give human happiness a firmer foundation than fickle fortune. If men can find no basis for

[2] II Corinthians iv. 16.

happiness except in their adjustment to external realities, they will not suffer pain to realize a kingdom of righteousness. If they are taught to identify physical well-being with their cherished peace, they will not venture farther than such actions as a cool prudence prompts. The cross was inspired by devotion to a "kingdom which is not of this world"; but the cross was also the method by which that kingdom was changed from an ethereal to a concrete reality. It is the absolute ideal which has no basis in concrete reality which moves men to defy the limitations of the concrete and overcome them. A religion which is perfectly at home in the world has no counsel for it which the world could not gain by an easier method.

Yet the reaction of modern religion to traditional other-worldliness is natural enough and, in a way, necessary. While religion cannot afford to discard its other-worldliness, the moral and social limitations which issue from it are obvious enough. We have previously observed the tendency of types of religion to withdraw the ideal from life and to imagine that it has magic potencies over life's realities, or that subjective devotion to it may absolve them of the duty of realizing it in history. All these defects are due to vagaries which are not inevitable characteristics of religious life. But the social limitations which result from the religious strategy of transcending the fortunes of life are constitutional and central. They therefore offer a very serious problem. If the soul is lifted above circumstances, it easily loses interest in changing them to better advantage. If its happiness is made independent of fortune, there is less purpose in making fortune secure. If personality discovers its highest satisfactions in defying environmental factors, it may become indifferent to the necessary projects of creating a more favorable environment for personal values. Human personality is an historic product, determined by specific forces of natural and social environment, and though it may attain its highest glory by transcending all circumstances, it will fall short if it adopts that strategy at the beginning and

[178]

not at the end of its efforts. The Orient, which produces more saints than the Occident, pays for them by the abject misery of its multitudes. Its highest moral achievements are really determined by a cruel law of survival. Only personalities of great spiritual resource can overcome the general physical conditions of its life which submerge the mass in hopeless poverty.

Some credit for the advantages of Western life must be given to the moral superiority of Christianity over Buddhism, which represents the quintessence of the Oriental spirit. Christianity is a life-affirming and Buddhism a life-denying faith. The one does not destroy but refines the energy of life. The other destroys energy in the process of refinement. The Orient is pantheistic; and by deifying all of life, offers no avenue of escape from its imperfections except by annihilation of life itself. There is a difference between fleeing to God from life's unbearable realities and identifying these with the divine will. At its worst the strategy of the Orient is a fatalistic acceptance of life's circumstances; at its best it is a stifling of all desires so that the soul may be free of the world. Yet there is a social peril even in the more wholesome strategy of Christianity which affirms life but divorces it from its physical necessities. This limitation is felt particularly when the conditions which invite change are social rather than natural. Nature is inexorable and it is well to learn that only they are able to escape her furies who also know how to renounce her delights. But the world which man has created retains its cruelties only by the sufferance of man. Anything which will incline men to assume an attitude of indifference toward projects of social reform and amelioration is therefore a potential peril to social progress. When Jesus rebuked the young man for his anxiety about an equitable division of his inheritance, he took a high spiritual ground which easily lends itself to abuse in the disillusioning realities of economic and social life. What if a sublime renunciation does not soften the hearts of those who hold more than their just share of the inheritance? And what if the welfare of others besides that of the moral idealist is involved in the renunciation? Shall the Biblical injunction to servants that they be obedient to their masters "not only to the good and gentle but also to the froward" apply to political tyrannies? Obviously an attitude which represents a high spiritual achievement in the individual instance has its limitations when raised to a general social policy. Social radicals who have been confronted with the conservatism of religion have parodied the other-worldly temper at the heart of this characteristic in the words: "Bye and bye, there'll be pie in the sky." The sneer in this parody hardly does justice to religious other-worldliness. The emphasis is not so much upon a future life as distinguished from the present existence as upon a type of life which can afford to regard "pie" with disdain whether in this or any other world. Nevertheless, even the highest type of other-worldliness may become the cause of indifference to social conditions. The very sensitiveness of religion which persuades it to regard human society in the same category with the world of nature as "the world" may result in the completer secularization of society and its abandonment to the unchecked forces of nature.

There is no easy formula for avoiding this social peril in the strategy of religion. The elimination of pantheism is a material aid in its solution. The superior energy of the West may be due to a tentative dualism in its religion which has been qualified from time to time by pantheistic and monistic thought but never completely destroyed. Yet even the dualism of Christianity does not save it altogether from positions which offer peril to social and moral values. Even an observer who is entirely sympathetic to religion must come to the conclusion that the West owes many of its advantages to the fact that religion has had no easy time in Western life, and that in the past centuries not only scientific thought but scientific life-strategy has challenged religion at every turn. Some of the excellencies of Western life are clearly the fruits of our science rather than our religion. Of course, these advantages have been bought at a price. The empirical instincts of science drive it to deny the continuities in reality and to see everything only in its momentary and immediate situation. The modern behavioristic destruction of the concept of personality is therefore one of the natural results of scientific thought betrayed into absurdity by its own consistency. But a consistent religion is generally equally absurd. Regarding all reality, and personality in particular, *sub specie æternitatis,* it fails to see how truly personality is the product of specific social and natural forces and neglects to change the material environment in the interest of human welfare. Human personality can be understood neither in terms of its environment alone nor in absolute terms which leave the material world in which it develops out of account. The final victory of personality must be gained by transcending concrete situations and material circumstances; but it is a hollow victory if circumstances are not previously used and amended to improve personal values. The soul is at once the victim and the master of the material world. It gains its highest triumph by renouncing the world, but the renunciation is premature if a futile and yet not futile effort is not made to make the natural world conform to the needs of human character.

While the Western world has much to learn from the East in its strategy of life, there is no gain in substituting one strategy for the other; for they are both defective. The plight of the West is due to the complete bankruptcy of religious forces and the unchallenged dominion of science; just as the plight of the East is due to the unchallenged sway of religion. Applied science has created a civilization which may be as destructive of personality for the meagerly endowed multitudes as the natural poverty of Asia. But Western civilization may at least boast of developing a middle class which enjoys physical and spiritual advantages which no considerable class of the Orient possesses. Neither the West nor the East has arrived at a perfect basis for happiness. The Oriental soul is like a bird, freed of its cage, but with no wings to fly. The Occidental soul has wings but is so fascinated by its gilded cage that it does not care to fly.

The conclusion which emerges from such reflections will shock orthodox religionists. It is that the values of religion are conditioned and not absolute and that they attain their highest usefulness not when they subdue all other values but when they are in perpetual conflict with them, or it may be truer to say when they are coördinated with them. Western life gained an advantage over the East by centuries of conflict between the religious and scientific strategy of life. It is losing the advantage by an excessive devotion to concrete interests and by the capitulation of religion. The supreme tragedy of history would be the not improbable armed conflict between West and East, with the Orient in a frenzy of resentment against the greed of the Occident and the Occident in a natural fear of the low living standards of Asia. Part of the truth would be on either side and the conflict could result only in exaggerating the limitations of the partial truth which each side holds.

Meanwhile there is the possibility of coördinating the values of East and West, of science and religion. Let the East learn to live in time and the West to view its temporalities with indifference. The coördination is not easy because men are not inclined to be at once critical and appreciative of the values with which they must deal. They always tend to increase the limitations of certain values by an uncritical devotion, or to destroy the values in mad resentment against their limitations. Since man is a citizen of two worlds, he cannot afford to renounce his citizenship in either. He must work out his destiny both as a child of nature and as a servant of the absolute.

The prospects for an exchange of values between the East and the West are not particularly bright. The Orient is indeed being "Americanized," but partly through the policy of Western imperialism exploiting the low living standards of Asia to the advantage of Western industry. There is no powerful movement in the West to dissuade it from its complete trust in physical power as the method of self-realization, and in physical comfort as the way to happiness. Modern religion has not been totally ineffective in qualifying racial arrogance and parochial prejudices. But it has had practically no effect upon the instincts of avarice which dominate Western life. The religious groups which are still ambitious to defy civilization in the name of their faith have a theology which cannot gain the respect of the thoughtful leaders of modern life; and the sins of which they convict modern society are not its real sins. The intellectually emancipated religious groups are too thoroughly acclimatized to the atmosphere of Western life to have any sensitiveness for its imperfections.

The greatest hope lies in the missionary enterprise, which through its very effort toward the universalization of the Christian faith has a tendency to strip it of its Occidental accretions, so that it may become intrinsically worthy of its world expansion. The missionary enterprise may thereby contribute as much toward the spiritualization of Western life as toward the regeneration of the East. Its very contact with the East gives it a perspective on the limitations of Western life which churches at home do not possess. There is, of course, the possibility that Western imperialism will so thoroughly discredit the missionary enterprise before it can function in this way that it will lose its whole prestige in the Eastern world. In that case Japan will probably continue to unify and occidentalize Asia in the hope of fighting fire with fire. A small minority of thoughtful missionaries are making a desperate effort to disassociate the missionary enterprise from the politics of Western imperialism in the Orient. Considering the difficulty of their task, they have made commendable progress. Yet if Christianity at home does not become disassociated from and does not qualify the greed of which the Oriental politics of Western nations is but one expression, the heroic efforts of the missionaries may be vain. Men of prudence in the Orient may be willing to concede that ideals have validity even if they are outraged by those who ostensibly accept them. But the final test of ideals must include their ability to qualify human action. If Christian idealism is to be a force which will help to create a unified world culture, capable of destroying the moral limitations of both the Oriental and the Occidental strategy of life, it must detach itself more completely from the temper of Western life even while it seeks to influence the thought of the East.

CHAPTER VIII

A PHILOSOPHICAL BASIS FOR AN ETHICAL
RELIGION

THE ethical problem of religion may be more important than the metaphysical one, as previously observed, but it cannot be solved without a reorientation of the present philosophical basis of religious conviction. The Western world has had a slight advantage over the East in the tentative dualism of Christianity, but this advantage has been lost by the inevitable drift toward pantheism in Western thought. Pantheistic tendencies are potential perils to moral values in practically all religions. By identifying God and the natural world they either persuade men to resign themselves to the inadequacies of nature, under the illusion that divine sanctity has rendered them immutable, or they blind the eye to the imperfections of nature and thus destroy the moral sensitiveness of religion. The Orient has usually derived a morally enervating pessimism from its pantheism, while the Occident has chosen the other horn of the monistic dilemma and fallen into a sentimental optimism. Both alternatives are as untrue to the facts as they are inadequate to men's moral needs.

In the Western world religious optimism has been gradually destroyed by the advance of science which discredited the moral over-estimate of the cosmic order, implicit as one of two tendencies in pantheism. The practical and tragic realities of its international and industrial life have added to the disillusionment and made men as sceptical of human as of cosmic virtue. Thus the cynicism of dis-illusioned intelligence is added to the despair of an outraged conscience to unite in a pessimism which questions both the rationality of the universe and the morality of man. The despair of the West is even more devastating to moral values than the pessimism of the East, for the Orient is prompted by its religion to a serene resignation while the West spends itself in blind fury or sensual excess. When all confidence in moral values is destroyed, the strong express themselves by asserting their power or resenting their seeming impotence, while the weak sink into an easy indulgence of natural appetites. The real history of Western society is being written by Nietzschian and Marxian cynics who have subdued every scruple which might qualify their contest for power. Meanwhile their conflict is lazily witnessed by vast hordes whose main purpose in life is to gratify their senses and who give their sympathy to one or the other side according as it offers least hindrance to their enjoyments. In such a situation religion is easily relegated to the position of restraining the petty and obscuring the major vices of the small minority which still profess it. This is particularly true when optimism and sentimentality, such as characterize modern religion, make it incapable of a realistic evaluation of the forces which reveal themselves in human society.

Albert Schweitzer [1] interprets the whole

---

[1] In *Civilization and Ethics* and *The Decay and Restoration of Civilization.*

moral bankruptcy of Western civilization as a pessimistic reaction to the extravagant optimism of its traditional religions and philosophies. While other factors, such as the complexity and the impersonal nature of industrial society, have been contributory factors to the disillusionment of the age, it is probably true that men are inclined to expect too little of the world and of man mostly because too much has been claimed for them and extravagant hopes have been disappointed. A regeneration of the ethical life of Western society must depend, therefore, upon the revival of a religion in which the Scylla of pantheism and the Charybdis of pure naturalism are avoided. While the Orient has a serenity which will contribute much to the art of living in a unified world civilization, there is no health for our sickness in its religious philosophies. Its pantheism cannot be maintained in the scientific atmosphere of the West, and if it could, as it is in rare instances, it would only present us with the impossible choice between the moral ennui of pessimism and the sentimentality of an unqualified optimism. The youthful exuberance of the Western mind invariably inclines it to the least defensible of these two bad alternatives, the optimistic one. When the West borrows religion from the East, as for instance in theosophy and Christian Science, it is used to support optimistic illusions so palpably absurd that they flourish only in those circles of society in which life is extremely comfortable and not too intelligent.

The only fruitful alternative to a monism and pantheism which identifies God and the world, the real and the ideal, is a dualism which maintains some kind of distinction between them and does not lose one in the other. Dualistic solutions to the riddles of life are not new in the history of religious thought. They are in fact as numerous as pantheistic ones, but their metaphysical limitations have usually outweighed their moral advantages and shortened their life. In Zoroastrianism, the noblest of purely Aryan faiths, Ahirman the spirit of evil exists independently of Ormuzd the good spirit. The influence of this Persian dualism

is seen in both Hebrew and Christian thought.
The satanology of the Old Testament is
partly derived from it; and Manichæism,
through which Augustine passed before he
embraced and elaborated Catholic orthodoxy,
is a compound of Persian and Christian
religion. Mythology is filled with efforts to do
justice to the conflicts which the world reveals
as obviously as its unities, as for instance in the
myth of Prometheus and Zeus. Even Plato,
from whom most Western pantheism has been
indirectly derived, held that God's perfect
goodness was thwarted by the intractableness
of the materials with which he worked.

Early Hebrew religion was naïvely dualistic,
and that is one reason why it has been so
potent in the history of religion. God was
indeed conceived of as omnipotent; that conception was the path that led to monotheism.
But the idea of omnipotence was elaborated
dramatically rather than philosophically. The
heavens might declare his glory and the firma-
ment show his handiwork, but he was revealed
in national history and (according to the concep-

tion of the later prophets) in personal experience more than in natural phenomena. Even a
very early prophet discovered that the still small
voice rather than the earthquake or the fire was
the symbol of his presence. The Genesis
account of the fall solves the problem of evil
upon an essentially monistic basis by making
human sin responsible for even the inadequacies of nature and attributing everything from
weeds to mortality to the luckless error of the
first man. Neither the goodness nor the omnipotence of God is abridged in this naïve but
sublime conception in which the human conscience assumes responsibility for more than its
share of human ills in order to save the reputation of divine virtue. The monism of this
account is, however, qualified by the injection
of the tempting serpent, an element which is
precursor of the belief in the devil, which the
Jews inherited from Babylonia and Persia and
which has fortunately qualified all monistic
tendencies in Jewish and Christian orthodoxy
until this day. A profounder instinct than
reveals itself to the casual observer persuades

fundamentalism to defend the reality of the devil with such vehemence. It may be metaphysically inconsistent to have two absolutes, one good and one evil, but the conception provides at least for a dramatic portrayal of the conflict which disturbs the harmonies and unities of the universe, and therefore, it has a practical and ethical value. The idea of attributing personality to evil may be scientifically absurd but it rests upon a natural error. When the blind and impersonal forces of nature come to life in man they are given the semblance of personality.

Professor Albert Schweitzer [2] ascribes the moral superiority of prophetic Juadism and Christianity over other world religions to the naïve dualism of the prophets and Jesus, who emphasized the moral rather than the metaphysical attributes of God in such a way as to develop a practical and morally potent distinction between God and the universe, between the ideal of religious devotion and the disappointing realities of life. The distinction

[2] *Christianity and Other World Religions.*

between Oriental monism and the practical dualism of Christianity in its unspoiled form is succinctly stated by Professor Alfred Whitehead: "Christianity has always been a religion seeking a metaphysics in contrast to Buddhism which is a metaphysics generating a religion. . . . The defect of a metaphysical system is the very fact that it is a neat little system which thereby oversimplifies its expression of the world. . . . In respect to its treatment of evil, Christianity is therefore less clear in its metaphysical idea but more inclusive of the facts." [3]

In the early Christian church the naïve dualism of Jesus was given dramatic and dynamic force through his deification, so that he became, in a sense, the God of the ideal, the symbol of the redemptive force in life which is in conflict with evil. Since no clear distinction was made between the spirit of the living Christ and the indwelling Holy Ghost, the doctrine of the trinity was, in effect, a symbol of an essential dualism. Orthodox Christian-

[3] *Religion in the Making*, page 50.

ity did indeed renounce the gnostic heresy
which tried to give this implicit dualism explicit
character by its distinction between the God
who was revealed in Jesus and the God of
creation. And history has justified the wisdom
of its course. The scientific precision necessary
to save such theology from essential polytheism
was lacking and Christianity was intent upon
guarding its monotheism. Yet it preserved
enough metaphysical inconsistency to retain
dualistic tendencies in its monistic orthodoxy.
Its symbols lacked philosophical precision but
they did give vivid and dramatic force to the
idea of a conflict between evil and the redemptive and creative force in life. Thus it could
fulfill the two great functions of religion
in prompting men to repent of their sins, and
in encouraging them to hope for redemption
from them. No mechanical or magical expla-
nations of the significance of the crucifixion
have ever permanently obscured the helpful
spiritual symbolism of the cross in which the
conflict between good and evil is portrayed and
the possibility as well as the difficulty of the

triumph of the good over evil is dramatized. An absolute dualism either between God and the universe or between man and nature, or spirit and matter, or good and evil, is neither possible nor necessary. What is important is that justice be done to the fact that creative purpose meets resistance in the world and that the ideal which is implicit in every reality is also in conflict with it. The reason why naïve religions are "more inclusive of the facts" in portraying this struggle than highly elaborated theologies is that the latter are always prompted by the rational need of consistency to obscure some facts for the sake of developing an intellectual plausible unity. Religions grow out of real experience in which tragedy mingles with beauty and man learns that the moral values which dignify his life are embattled in his own soul and imperiled in the world. He is inclined neither to obscure the reality of the struggle nor to sacrifice the hope of victory until too much reflection persuades him to believe either that all partial evil is universal good or that destiny makes his struggle futile and his defeat inevitable. That is how morality dies with religion when an age has become too sophisticated.

Naïve Christianity was unable to maintain itself in the Græco-Roman world without making concessions to its intellectual scruples and paying for its conquests by incorporating Hellenic philosophies in its theology. The gospel was diluted with neo-Platonism to make it more palatable for a cultured world. The naïvely and dramatically conceived omnipotence of God was metaphysically elaborated and inevitably betrayed the church into an essential pantheism, which "turns the natural world, man's stamping-ground and system of opportunities, into a self-justifying and sacred life, endows the blameless giant with an inhuman soul and worships the monstrous divinity it has fabricated." [4] The process of compounding the simplicities of the gospel with the dialectic achievements of Greek philosophy culminated in St. Augustine who laid the foundation for Christian orthodoxy and made

[4] George Santayana in *Religion and Reason*, page 176.

the simple Christian epic the basis of an elaborate theological structure in which God
becomes at the same time the guarantee of the
reality of the ideal and the actual cause of every
concrete reality. Christianity has always
anathematized pantheism officially, but probably—as Professor Santayana suggests—
because it suspected that it was a suppressed
but not entirely quiescent half of its dogma.
Vital religion has a way of expressing itself
outside the limits of its rationally fixed concepts and the essential pantheism of orthodox
Christianity therefore did not destroy the
moral vigor of even such resolute determinists
as Augustine or John Calvin. Yet in the end
the logic of a system of ideas becomes the pat-
tern of human action. A rigorous determinism
as well as an unqualified pantheism destroys
moral vigor because it either makes the attainment of the ideal too certain or idealizes the
real beyond all evidence. If reality only thinly
veils the ideal implicit in it, or if the implicit
ideal is certain to become real in history, there
is no occasion for moral adventure and no

reason for moral enthusiasm. In a sense pantheism is naturalism with an unnatural light upon it. That is why the determinism implied in pantheism may lead so easily to a reaction of naturalistic determinism. Thus Karl Marx appropriated Hegel's determinism and put it to his own use. When the whole wealth of Hegel's dialectical skill served no better purpose than to deify the Prussian military state, as a kind of ultimate revelation of the counsels of God, it was easy enough to discredit its optimistic illusions without destroying its determinism. The residual determinism became the basis of a new philosophy of history in which natural instinct and economic necessity took the place of divine will as man's inexorable fate. The reaction from Hegel to Marx is a perfect symbol of the whole course of Western thought in the last hundred years with its change from a supernatural to a naturalistic determinism.

Religion left to itself, even when it elaborates theologies, tries to do some justice to the reality of moral conflict even though it may

[203]

confuse the issue by a faulty definition of divine omniptoence. But its necessary coöperation with metaphysics drives it inevitably into more and more consistent monisms in which moral enthusiams are destroyed. The monistic and pantheistic element in Western religion was greatly increased by its intimate collaboration with philosophies which dealt chiefly with the problem of knowledge. For the solution of the epistemological problem the philosophical idealists thought it necessary to posit an all-knowing intelligence. It was this all-knowing absolute which became the support of religion's faith in God against the attacks of realists and empiricists, though there was little enough affinity between the God of any healthy religious theism and the impersonal absolute of monistic philosophers.

When religious apologists found it necessary to readjust the age-old affirmations of faith to the evolutionary facts revealed by science they usually sank even more deeply into the morass of pantheistic and monistic philosophy. The old and naïve conceptions of a capricious om-

nipotence working its will upon natural phenomena became manifestly untenable and a
way had to be found to relate divine purpose
to and discover the area of creativity in the
natural and cosmic processes. It was practically inevitable that such a task would be accomplished only by an overemphasis on divine
immanence and a consequent betrayal of
religion into a sentimental optimism. When
defenders of religious faith were borrowing
from the quiver of their opponents they would
have done well to consult Thomas Huxley
more and Herbert Spencer less; for Huxley
was morally much more realistic than Spencer.
Spencerian doctrines lent themselves more
easily to the strategy of linking religious
theism with the faith of science in the dependability of the universe; but there was something
lacking in Spencerian optimism which is very
vital to religion, a sense of the tragic in life
and an awareness of the frustration which
moral purpose and creative will must meet
in nature and in man. The sentimentality of
modern religion is of course older than the

optimism which it derived from Spencer. Part of it is derived from Rousseau and the romanticism of the eighteenth century. Here again religion suffered the fate of snatching error while it was borrowing truth from its opponents. Renouncing the idea of total depravity which was central in medieval religion, and in orthodox Protestantism for that matter, it evolved a sentimental over-estimate of human virtue which is no nearer the truth than the medieval conceptions of original sin. It is a strange irony in history that to-day irreligion, in the form of deter-ministic psychology, should elaborate doctrines strangely akin to the derogatory estimates of human resources made by medieval theologians. So modern churches are involved in an opti-mistic overestimate of the virtue of both man and nature at the very time when science tempts men to despair of discovering moral integrity in the one and moral meaning in the other. Modern religion is, in short, not suffi-ciently modern. In it eighteenth-century sentimentality and nineteenth-century individualism are still claiming victory over the ethical and religious prejudices of the Middle Ages. Meanwhile life has moved on and the practical needs of modern society demand an ethic which is not individualistic and a religion which is not unqualifiedly optimistic.

The practical effects of this lack of contact of modern religion with the real temper of modern life may be gauged by comparing the observations of any average denominational journal of religion upon the events of contemporary history with the realistic analyses of secular journals. The brutalities of the economic conflict, the disillusioning realities of international relations, the monstrous avarice of nations and the arrogance of races, all these sins with which the life of modern society is cursed are treated with an easy complacency by religious observers which contrasts strangely with the frantic anxiety of secular idealists. In a recent world conference of the churches at Stockholm members of the German delegation objected to what they regarded as an identification of the Kingdom of God with the

League of Nations made by a good bishop in the opening sermon. National prejudice may have prompted this criticism but the superior perspective lent by bitter experience gave it a measure of justification, and it would be applicable to other sermonic interpretations of current history besides those of the bishop.

The war itself was a disheartening revelation of the moral obfuscation of modern religion when dealing with the tragedies of history. The easy partnership of religious sentiment with patriotic fervor has been previously ascribed to the natural relation between religion and any devotion to an ethical ideal, however imperfect. There is, however, yet another reason for the blindness of religious idealists to the horrors of war. The monistic orientation of modern religion made it necessary for the church to save religious faith by discovering the saving virtues in the great evil. It was therefore unable to view the realities in proper proportion. For a realistic interpretation of the great tragedy modern society had to depend upon secular idealists who did not feel called upon to save either God's or man's reputation.

Sentimentality is a poor weapon against cynicism, and idealistic determinism has no way of defeating determinism of the naturalistic type. Since both the latter represent reactions to the former, they can be overcome only by bringing these into closer conformity with the facts. The freedom and moral integrity of man is not an illusion but it is a fact very seriously circumscribed. Transcendent purpose and creative will in the universe may be scientifically validated but do not thereby become the effective cause of every natural phenomenon. What is needed is a philosophy and a religion which will do justice both to the purpose and to the frustration which purpose meets in the inertia of the concrete world, both to the ideal which fashions the real and to the real which defeats the ideal, both to the essential harmony and to the inevitable conflict in the cosmos and in the soul. In a sense there is not a single dualism in life; rather there are many of them. In his own life man may experience a conflict between his moral will and the anarchic desires with which nature has endowed him; or he may experience a conflict between his cherished values and the caprices of nature which know nothing of the economy of values in human life. In the cosmic order the conflict is between creativity and the resistance which fustrates creative purpose. Whether the dualism is defined as one of mind and matter, or thought and extension, or force and inertia, or God and the devil, it approximates the real facts of life. It may be impossible to do full justice to the two types of facts by any set of symbols or definitions; but life gives the lie to any attempt by which one is explained completely in terms of the other. There is no more reason to-day to deny the reality of God than to explain every casual phenomenon in terms of his omnipotent will.

Our interest is in the moral fruits of religious and philosophical ideas rather than in their perfect consistency, but it may be noted in passing that philosophically competent scientists and scientifically competent philosophers arrive at conclusions to-day which are in closer accord with a naïve theism than with the monism of absolute idealism. They do not of course picture a God who is outside of the world and at work upon it as a potter upon his clay; but they do justice to both the purpose and the limitation of purpose in the creative process. Professor Hobhouse writes: "The evolutionary process can best be understood as the effect of a purpose slowly working itself out under limiting conditions which it brings successively under control. . . . This would mean not that reality is spiritual or the creation of an unconditioned mind . . . but that there is a spiritual element integral to the structure and movement of reality and that evolution is the process by which this principle makes itself master of the residual conditions which at first dominate its life and thwart its efforts." [5] It may be a natural overbelief and an inevitable anthropomorphism if religion attributes all the characteristics of personality to the purpose,

[5] In *Development and Purpose,* page 360.

"the spiritual element integral to the structure and movement of reality." But if a place for freedom and purpose in the cosmic order, however conditioned, is discovered the essential affirmation of religious faith is metaphysically verified. The values of personality are related to cosmic facts. Professor Alfred Whitehead defines God as that in reality which is not concrete but the principle of every concrete actuality. He makes the telling observation that while a dynamic view of reality may dispense with God as the prime mover it must substitute for Aristotle's prime mover a principle of limitation and concretion, since the dynamic nature of reality does not account for the various forms in which it is made concrete.* In other words the faith of religion in both the transcendence and immanence of God is given a new metaphysical validation. His unchangeableness is "his self-consistency in relation to all change"; but this does not justify the deterministic conclusion of a "complete self-con-

* In *Religion in the Making*.

sistency of the temporal world." The reality
of God and the reality of evil as a positive
force are thus both accepted.

There is, in short, no reason why religion
should not hold to its faith in God without
either identifying him with or losing him in
the concrete world. The moral and spiritual
values in which religion is interested have a
basis in concrete actuality. They are on the
one hand not a mere effervescence on the sur-
face of the concrete, and on the other hand
they are not the only basis of historical realities. The pluralism of William James, which
has been criticized as scientifically inac-
curate and metaphysically inconsistent, seems
to have both scientific and metaphysical
virtues. There is good reason to accept
at least a qualified dualism not only because
it is morally more potent than traditional
monisms, but because it is metaphysically
acceptable. It is not to be expected that
science will ever invest the concept of God with
the attributes which religious devotion assigns

to it. But there is no reason why religious and moral experience should not build further upon the foundation laid by science. It is manifestly necessary to have some metaphysical basis for religious conviction, for there is no spiritual vigor in the conscious self-deception of purely subjective religions. But it is not necessary to limit religion to the bare concepts which science establishes. It is in fact better for religion to forego perfect metaphysical consistency for the sake of moral potency. In a sense religion is always forced to choose between an adequate metaphysics and an adequate ethics. That is not to say that the two interests are incompatible but that they are not identical. When there is a conflict between them it is better to leave the metaphysical problem with some loose ends than to develop a religion which is inimical to moral values. The reason why naïve religions have frequently been morally more potent than highly rationalized ones is not because the faith which gave them moral fervor was necessarily inconsistent with the facts, but because they based their affirmations upon facts and experiences which were inconsistent with each other or seemed to be but were equally true and equally necessary for the maintenance of moral and spiritual energy.

The objection to religious dualism comes not only from those who subordinate all advantages to that of rational consistency but also from those who believe that it imperils purely religious values. It robs God of omnipotence (so the argument runs) and the universe of dependability. It gives no certain guarantee of the triumph of personal and spiritual values. It may put a note of challenge in religion, but it also destroys its comforting assurances. The answer to such a criticism is that the moral virtues of dualism are derived from precisely that characteristic. It is not easy to challenge to conflict and to guarantee victory at one and the same time. By dignifying personality religion runs the peril of obscuring the defects of human nature; if it makes the triumph of righteousness certain, it may incline men to take "moral holidays."

Too much emphasis upon the harmonies of the universe may make evil seem unreal. If men are given the opportunity, they will extract comfort from religion and forget the challenge implied in its faith; which simply means that they will use religion to sublimate rather than to qualify their will to live. They will accept the assurance of faith that the frustrations of the natural world are not permanent, but they will not accept the challenge of faith to overcome the corruptions of nature in their own souls.

The perennial conflict between priest and prophet is given in the double function of religion. The priest dispenses comfort and the prophet makes the challenge of religion potent. The priest is more numerous than the prophet because human selfishness is as determining in religion as in other fields. Though the priest always defeats the prophet in the end, the prophet is avenged because his original experience is the reality which makes the priest's assurance plausible. There is no way of guaranteeing the reality of God if someone does not make him real in experience, and there is no way of declaring the victory of the ideal if someone does not defeat reality in the name of the ideal in history. Religion validates itself in spiritual experience and moral triumph. Speculation and deduction contribute to religious certainty only after experience has laid the foundation for faith. It is not possible to free religion altogether of its priestly corruptions. But anything which will make it more difficult to accept the comforts of faith without accepting its challenges will increase the moral potency of religion and decrease the possibility of its corruption by those who want to use it for the purpose of insuring the dignity of human life without paying the price of moral effort for the boon.

There is no reason why the comforting assurances of religion should be sacrificed completely. Science is not inimical to the assumption of religion that personal and moral values have a basis in the universe itself which insures their permanence and their further refinement. Though God works his will against the inertia of the concrete world and the waywardness of man, neither science nor history justifies the conclusion that his resources are not ultimately equal to the creative task. The intractableness of the world makes the creative and redemptive struggle real but not hopeless. Religion has as much right to preach hope as it has to preach repentance. It fails in its task if it does not save men from despair as well as from undue pride and complacency. There is nothing in either science or history which invalidates either function of religion. But science unites with moral experience in insisting on the reality and the painfulness of the creative process in man and in nature. If the resistance to moral purpose in cosmic history is underestimated, it merely serves to increase that resistance in the life of man by justifying his moral inertia. The needs of a dynamic religion are consistent with scientific fact, though not always compatible with a completely consistent metaphysics. Science may well combine with religion in persuading man that "if hopes are dupes, fear may be liars," and that he must "work out his salvation with fear and trembling."

CHAPTER IX

At the risk of unnecessary repetition it may
be well to capitulate the most important conclusions which emerge from our study of
religion in contemporary civilization. Religion
is dying in modern civilization not only because
it has not yet been able to restate its affirmations so that they will be consistent with scientific fact, but also because it has not been able
to make its ethical and social resources available for the solution of the moral problems of
modern civilization. Its rejuvenation therefore waits upon a reorientation of its ethical
traditions as well as of its theological conceptions. It is under the necessity of finding some
metaphysical basis for its personalization of
the universe, but its scientific and philosophical
respectability will be of no avail if the moral
fruits which issue from its affirmations and

experiences do not actually qualify the brute struggle of life, so largely determined by natural forces.

Religion is scientifically verified if freedom and purpose are found to have a place in the cosmic processes, and it is ethically justified if it helps to create and maintain creative freedom and moral purpose in human life. The present moral impotence of Protestant Christianity is partially derived from the inadequacy of some of its traditions which it inherited out of periods of history which had different moral needs than our own day. Its individualism rendered a universal service at the dawn of the modern era but survives to-day chiefly as a sanctification of the peculiar interests and prejudices of one particular class in Western society. The limitations of its ethical traditions are easily obscured not only because all religion easily gives the semblance of finality to the relativities of history, but because a religion which imagines itself devoted to the spirit of Jesus is under the temptation of exploiting the prestige of his absolute

ethics without approximating his ethical position.

The moral effectiveness of religion depends
upon its ability to detach itself from the historical relativities with which its ideals are
inevitably compounded in the course of history.
The avowed loyalty of the Christian church to
the spirit of Christ may become the basis of
such a detachment, since there is little in the
gospel of Jesus which conforms to the dominant interests of modern life. But the very
reverence in which Jesus is held may operate
to obscure the essential genius of his life.
Religion is therefore under the necessity of
developing the critical faculty even while it
maintains its naïvete and reverence. The
necessity of coöperation between the naturally
incompatible factors of reason and imagination,
of intelligence and moral dynamic, is really the
crux of the religious and moral problem in
modern civilization. The complexity of modern life demands that moral purpose be
astutely guided; but moral purpose itself is
rooted in ultra-rational sanctions and may be

destroyed by the same intelligence which is needed to direct it. Both humility and love, the highest religious virtues, are ultra-rational; yet they cannot be achieved in an intricate social life without a discriminating intelligence which knows how to uncover covert sins and to discover potential virtues. The incidental limitations which every historic type of religion reveals can be dealt with only if the religious devotee can be persuaded to regard the values of his religion critically; yet the cultivation of such a critical spirit may easily lead to the enervation of the religious spirit itself. If the highest values of religion are themselves conditioned rather than absolute, it must be possible to assign them a place in the hierarchy of values, without encouraging a complete loss of confidence in them. Such a task is difficult but not impossible. A robust moral idealism will help to create a spiritual fervor which will not be easily defeated by any superficial intellectualism. If institutions of religion gave preference to the ethical rather than the intellectual problem of religious faith, it might be

[223]

possible to create a religious spirit sufficiently vigorous to permit the free play of the critical faculties without a loss of moral or spiritual dynamic. Obviously civilization cannot afford to dispense with either the irrational moral will or the critical intelligence by which it is made effective in complex situations. Men need to subject all partial moral achievements to comparison with the absolute standards of truth, beauty and goodness of their religious faith, and yet be able to see and willing to concede the relativities in the absolute values of their devotion. They can be saved from a morality of mere utilitarianism only by the religious quest for an absolute moral standard; yet they need to be discerning enough to see that every ethical achievement, even when inspired by religious motives, is tinged with prudential self-interest. They must continue to strive after freedom and yet realize that human life and character is largely determined by environment. If they seek happiness, divorced from fortune, they nevertheless cannot escape the duty of making the material world serve human

welfare. Their ability to discover the transcendent values in human personality has value
only if they maintain faith in human nature
after they have discovered its imperfections.
They must search after the perfect goodness
in God and yet be prepared to face the cruelties of life without either denying their reality
or being driven to despair by them.

If it is true that moral sincerity is even more
necessary to a vital religion in modern life than
intellectual modernity, a strategy must be
developed to sever religious idealism from the
unethical tendencies in modern civilization.
Any strategy which will succeed in such an
enterprise will savor of asceticism. The limitations of historic asceticism may teach the
present how to avoid inevitable pitfalls in the
task of detaching religious idealism from the
corruptions of society. An asceticism which
flees the world and develops its saints at the
price of abandoning industrial civilization even
more completely to the natural and anarchic
forces which operate in its life, is obviously of
no use to modern civilization. Yet a type of

asceticism is needed, if for no other reason, because greed is the dominant motive of Western civilization and nothing less than an ascetic discipline will free religious idealism from its entanglement with the covetousness of modern life. Since Western life is intent upon material advantages, no religious idealism can maintain any degree of purity if it does not enter into a conscious conflict with the civilization in which it functions and succeed in setting some bounds to the expansive desires of men and of nations.

The church as such has sufficient spiritual resources to become the recruiting ground for such a movement of detachment, but it is too much to hope that it will take the leadership in it. It is too deeply enmeshed with the interests and prejudices of contemporary civilization to possess the insight and courage which the enterprise requires. Such a movement of detachment must be, as it has always been, a minority movement. But the minority ought not detach itself from the majority so completely that it will sacrifice the possibility of acting as a leaven in it. There is no force or strategy which can prevent the great majority from using religion to give human personality dignity and self-respect without a serious effort to approximate a moral ideal which would justify religion's estimate of human worth. Some types of religion will continue to obscure the defects in nature and human nature. They will reassure the perplexed soul by recounting the victories of the past without seeking new triumphs. They will build systems of faith upon past experiences without any effort to validate or amend them in fresh experience. Thus rejuvenation and progress must come from the few who understand the fuller implications of the faith which they share with the multitudes whose eyes are holden and who lack the courage to follow even such visions as may come to them.

A highly spiritual religion cannot be an esoteric possession to which the multitudes may never aspire. It cannot afford to lose confidence in the multitudes; yet it must resist the gravitation toward moral mediocrity among them. It certainly must avoid the cultivation of a priestly cult into which the layman cannot be initiated. If the modern movement of detachment is to be effective it must in fact be a layman's movement; for it must express itself in rebuilding the social order rather than in building new religious institutions. Its most effective ministers will be laymen who will lack neither the technical skill nor the spiritual resource to deal with the practical problems of industry and politics. Religious teachers may help to inspire such a movement, but its efficacy will depend upon those who are engaged in the world's work. If the greed of Western civilization is to be qualified by religious idealism, it will be accomplished by men who use and direct the machines of modern industry without making mechanical efficiency an end in itself and without succumbing to the lure of the material rewards which come so easily to those who are proficient in the industrial enterprise. A revival of either puritan or monastic asceticism will be unequal to the task which faces modern religion. Puritanism sanc-

tified economic power, and monasticism fled its
responsibilities. The new asceticism must produce spiritualized technicians who will continue
to conquer and exploit nature in the interest
of human welfare, but who will regard their
task as a social service and scorn to take a
larger share of the returns of industry than is
justified by reasonable and carefully scrutin-
ized needs. The new asceticism must, in short,
be in the world and yet not of the world. It
must be truly scientific in gauging the advantage to human personality in the conquest of
nature and truly religious in finding a basis
for human happiness beyond the material
rewards which this conquest returns.

If Christian idealists are to make religion
socially effective they will be forced to detach
themselves from the dominant secular desires
of the nations as well as from the greed of
economic groups. The socially minded portion
of the church has in fact made some progress
in this direction. The lessons of the World
War have not been altogether futile, and there
is a wholesome mood of repentance in the

church for its easy connivance with an unethical nationalism in the past centuries. The church has not yet had an opportunity to prove the sincerity of its contrition in this matter, for the moment of crisis has not yet come. In that moment, which will come inevitably, many religiously inspired peace idealists will no doubt bow their knees to Baal; but there is real reason to hope that there is a new conscience in the church which will resist the claims of an unethical nationalism to the utmost. Perhaps the greatest weakness of the religious idealists who have become critical of an unethical nationalism is that they are not sufficiently aware of the intimate and organic relation between the imperialism of nations and the whole tendency of avarice which characterizes Western life. Too few realize that it is not possible to detach oneself from an unethical nationalism if one continues to enjoy the material advantages which flow from the nation's unqualified insistence upon the right to hold its advantages against the world. It may be impossible to arrive at a complete equalization of living standards among all individuals who desire to achieve and express the ideal of the brotherhood of man. But a religious idealism which does not move in that direction will be convicted of insincerity and moral confusion. Unrepentant political realists may well pour contempt upon it and justly accuse those who profess it of profiting from policies which they ostensibly condemn. Religious idealism is in desperate need of a strategy which will express its detachment from the dominant desires and impulses of modern civilization by something more than desultory and usually qualified criticism of unethical political ideals and industrial policies.

The old challenge "be ye not conformed to this world" must be accepted anew in a more heroic fashion than is customary in enlightened religious circles. The policy of building a Kingdom of God by regenerating individual lives has become discredited, not because moral character is dispensable to a wholesome social life, but because the criteria of moral character have been too individualistic to serve the needs of modern society. It is important enough that men gain some control over their immediate desires and discipline their momentary passions. Society is always in need of integrated personalities. But the validity of the religious ideal must finally be judged by its capacity to create not only unified personalities but personalities which know how to restrain their expansive desires for the sake of social peace. Religion intensifies selfishness when it adds sanctity to a respectable selfish life and creates a self-respect which is impervious to emotions of contrition. If the religious ideal is to gain any potency in modern life it must be able to convict men of sin and inspire them to a conversion. But the sins of which they need most to be convicted are those which are covert in the social and economic relations which custom has hallowed; and the conversion of life which is most needed is that which will express itself in terms of the economic and political relationships in which men live. Not to be conformed to this world, if it is to have any real meaning in modern life, will mean that the religiously inspired soul knows how to defeat the avarice and to overcome the indifference to the worth of human personality which inheres in the whole economic and industrial structure of modern society. Practically and individually such a detachment from the world will express itself in the sacrifice of material advantages for the sake of realizing a more intimate fellowship with the underprivileged, in the careful analysis of industrial policies from the standpoint of their effect upon personality, in an unwillingness to profit by social and economic practices and policies which are fundamentally unethical and in a willingness to bear some pain for the sake of expressing loyalty to the community of mankind as against all lesser and conflicting loyalties.

The hope of persuading any large number of religious people to express their spiritual convictions in any such socially tangible and revolutionary terms is made rather desperate by the fact that the modern church seems no more inclined to undertake the task of spiritual regeneration than the orthodox church. The orthodox church still possesses some of the religious fervor which is required to defy the world, but it is too anti-rational in its theology to gain the respect of the intelligent classes and too individualistic in its ethics to express religious idealism in socially helpful terms. The modern churches are not acutely conscious of any serious defects in contemporary civilization. If they do recognize limitations in the social order, they give themselves to the pleasant hope that time and natural progress will bring inevitable triumph to every virtuous enterprise. They have relegated the eschatological note of the gospel, by which Jesus expressed his sense of the tragic, to the limbo of theological antiquities. The possibility of a catastrophe seems never to arouse their fears or to give energy to their ambitions. Life, according to their gospel, goes automatically from grace to grace and from strength to strength.

Though neither the orthodox nor the modern wing of the Christian church seems capable of initiating a genuine religious revival which will evolve a morality capable of challenging and maintaining itself against the dominant desires of modern civilization and yet expressing itself in terms relevant to civilization's needs, there are resources in the Christian religion which make it the inevitable basis of any spiritual regeneration of Western civilization. Christianity, as Dr. Ernst Troeltsch has observed, is the fate of Western society. Spiritual idealisms of other cultures and societies may aid it in reclaiming its own highest resources; and any universal religion capable of inspiring an ultimately unified world culture may borrow from other religions. But the task of redeeming Western society rests in a peculiar sense upon Christianity. It is congenial to the energy and activism of Western peoples and is yet capable of setting bounds to their expansive desires. It has reduced the eternal conflict between self-assertion and self-denial to the paradox of self-assertion through self-denial and made the cross the symbol of life's highest achievement. Its optimism is rooted in pessimism and it is therefore able to preach both repentance and hope. It is able to condemn the world without enervating life and to create faith without breeding illusions. Its adoration of Jesus sometimes obscures the real genius of his life but cannot permanently destroy the fruitfulness of his inspiration. If there is any lack of identity between the Jesus of history and the Christ of religious experience, the Jesus of history is nevertheless more capable of giving historical reality to the necessary Christ idea than any character of history. Intelligence will gradually soften prejudices and allay the conflict between Christianity and the Judaism out of which it emerged and with which it is organically related so that the religions of the prophetic ideal may make common cause. Such a coöperation will probably never lead to complete fusion because Christianity cannot afford to sacrifice the Christ idea and the Jews will continue to regard this as a Hellenistic and unacceptable element in the Christian religion. Christianity will not disavow it, for it gives dramatic force and historical concretion to its theism and dualism. The God of our devotion is veritably revealed most adequately in the most perfect personality we know, as he is potentially revealed in all personal values; and his conflict with the inertia of the concrete and historical world is expressed most vividly in the cross of Christ. When dealing with life's ultimates, symbolism is indispensable, and a symbolism which has a basis in historic incident is most effective. The idea of a potent but yet suffering divine ideal which is defeated by the world but gains its victory in the defeat must remain basic in any morally creative world view.

It is possible of course that the resources of the Christian religion will not be made available in time to save Western civilization from moral bankruptcy. It is possible that life will continue to run its course of conflict between the unrestrained ambitions and desires of individuals and groups until unqualified self-assertiveness will issue in mutual destruction. It is possible that cynicism will continue to discount the moral potentialities of human nature while science continues to give plausibility to a depreciation of the moral factors in life by arming the brute in man and making his vices more deadly. Civilization may be beyond moral redemption; but if it is to be redeemed a religiously inspired moral idealism must aid in the task. A purely naturalistic ethics will not only be overcome by a sense of frustration and sink into despair, but it will lack the force to restrain the self-will and self-interest of men and of nations. If life cannot be centered in something beyond nature, it will not be possible to lift men above the brute struggle for survival. Intelligence may mitigate its cruelties and prudence may prompt men to eliminate its worst inhumanities; but the increased power which the conquest of nature supplies merely substitutes unintended cruelties for those which have been consciously abolished. Living on the naturalistic level men are bound to contend for life's physical prizes and to use physical force in the contest with more and more deadly effect.

It is the virtue of a vital religious idealism

that it lifts life above the level of nature and makes the development of an ethical personality the ultimate goal of human existence. Without the vivid and realistic other-worldly hopes and fears with which the medieval church disciplined life and which the modern church cannot restore, it may seem that religion possesses no force which could counteract the primitive impulses which move men and nations. But these hopes and fears were merely crude ways of expressing the idea that life is fundamentally moral and that its destiny transcends the animal conflict. Life will continue to develop in the direction of the ideal implicit in it and every organism is impelled to move toward the goal of its own completeness. The ideal implicit in human character is that of ethical freedom; and awakened personalities will seek to realize that ideal. They will seek to realize it even at the expense of physical sacrifices and pain. They will learn how to find life by losing it. It is the quest for what is not real but is always becoming real, for what is not true but is always becoming true, that makes man incurably religious. Modern religion is therefore not without resource in contending against the forces of nature. The great difficulty is that the struggle for ethical integrity is so painful that most men are tempted to seek some short-cut to it; and organized religion generally expresses the hopes and desires of this easygoing multitude. In the medieval church magic provided the short-cut. In the modern church it is provided by a sanctified prudence which teaches men how to be unselfish and selfish at the same time, how to gain moral self-respect without sacrificing too many temporal advantages. The hope of a revival of ethical religion and of an ethical reconstruction of society therefore depends, as it did in the past, upon a renunciation of the religious short-cuts which lead to hypocrisy.

If religious aspiration can be united with perfect moral sincerity a fruitful partnership may again be established between religion and morality. The moral struggle will give meaning to the affirmations of religion and the